"The Wealthy Farmer Diary"

By David S. Brown

Edited By JoA' Zuberi/Crumbs Publishing

"The majority of the testimonies at the front of this book are from people we've just met who upon reading "The Wealthy Farmer Diary" were touched to respond and we pray you will do the same as well, may God continually Bless you!"

Printed by Sportswood Printing

1

This book is
Dedicated to my
precious Father-In-Law
(my biggest mentor in this life)

C. William (Bill) Ferguson
who I know went to
be with the Lord
on July 2, 2006.

Testimonies

"From people we just met, who we consider to be friends."

What a fantastic read!! Your story has enlightened my heart. I started a notebook to jot down how I've been pushing and controlling others. There is so much I have thought about after the first reading, I will re-read it several times more. I have thanked God He has sent you our way. He sends us gifts, if we only open our eyes and minds to see them. I have asked Sharon to call the next time you are in town as I would like to introduce myself, for the computer seems rather cold and impersonal. I hope all is well with you and your family. May the Peace of Christ be with you!

Christopher Radford

Wow! You certainly have had a lot of dramatic experiences for teachers in your life-the 3-D's-nothing subtle. You must have been a "hard nut to crack" with regards to letting go of pride, but you did it and are sharing it with the world to help others. Many people go through life and don't learn their lessons along the way.

I ask why is this happening to me, sometimes again and again, and what lesson am I to learn from this. The biggest lesson for me is to think abundance and not lack. I believe what you think about… you get. I certainly feel and identify with your graphic stories regarding debt!

I meditate and write intentions every morning for 20 minutes and have been doing this for a year today as I started last February 1st. I was debating whether to continue after a year but after reading your book I will definitely continue. I modify what I do as I learn new material.

Bob McNaughton

It is possible and so easy for anyone to make a mistake. But not all can openly admit them. That takes a real person with real courage and strength. For you to tell that you drove while intoxicated, getting into a bad car wreck and causing your loved one serious back injuries, that takes a lot of courage just to admit what you did and then that it was wrong done to those you loved. Thank God she is alive and not paralyzed.

Drinking and driving is something that brings back memories for me. At around age 5, I remember riding in a big brown Buick; I'm in the front seat between my mother and her boyfriend, in the middle of winter, adding we are on the highway. My mother's boyfriend has a bottle of beer in between his legs, taking big gulps of beer in between drags of his cigarette, I remember being so scared, I thought for sure I was not going to make it home safely. Why would someone do this to themselves let alone a young child, I truly admire your courage and strength to admit what you've done wrong David, especially putting it out there for others to read that you don't even know. I believe your book will not only inspire people but will also give them a sense of forgiveness and maybe even closure. Your book will help them feel better about themselves and help them grow into being a better person.

Your book has really made me think about writing my story. Maybe I can help change some lives with my words too.

Thanks David,
What an inspiring book all around!

Jamie Girodat

Wow… I'm sitting at work right now and must admit that I committed the time, this time to read the latest draft because I really didn't want to do "work." It has been a very long and testing week. My best friend in the entire world delivered her new son yesterday, only 31 weeks along. I have spent much time this week in reflection and prayer. Everyone's first reaction including that of my friend and her husband (both strong believers) was that they were being punished for something. They had done everything worldly right. She had been healthy until last weekend, the baby too. No one could understand why this was happening. As her husband and I prayed with her at Mac Master, where she had been airlifted from the hospital in Alliston on the weekend, I looked at him and said: "Remember, He never gives you anything you can't handle." He smiled and hugged me, and yesterday "We" have a beautiful baby "Boy", breathing on his own with a little bit of oxygen crying eyes open and truly a blessing. This morning I am exhausted, thankful and now with a renewed sense of exactly why these things happen. Thank you seems… inadequate!

Jackie McKenzie

We have a lot in common, I too work on self-esteem issues of loving myself; 2007 is my year of being good to myself and loving myself and becoming the servant that God wants me to be. I live to please Him! I live to hear His Voice. I know what it is like to be knocked off my high horse, it happened when my dad died. Also, I have had more rejection than anyone I know from family and friends. I just found out that even my son has a hard time believing some of my stories, (and I am his mother).

   I know that the Blessings of Abraham, Isaac, and Jacob are with you. God Bless your new book!!

In His Service

Connie A. Sotomayor

Dear David

   As your message states this has been a labor of love. Without "Love" you probably would not have been able to share with everyone what has transpired during your lifetime to date. This has been wonderful to read and makes one "Stop and

think" where they have been. I'm sure this book will help
many to look deep into their hearts, admit their weaknesses and make necessary changes in their lives.
Congratulations!

Linda Corbett

I finally finished your book last night what a life God signed you up for and the lessons you've learned along the way. Because you got right down to the "nitty gritty" of dialogue there are many realizations I had in my own life. I am able to write down even the smallest thing and analyze it but I find that when you talk to others about this, they really don't want to hear. At times I almost found myself "hiding" from what you were going to reveal next. How could things get worse I would ask? How are things going to improve for this great guy who has just taken a dead-end road? I think that when we age to our 50's a red light flashes before us. A wand is waved and we start to race at getting things right that we think are wrong. It is as if we are fighting the clinical clock and the war on aging. We want a better life and we see successful people around us. We want what they have even if it is just their sanity. Some people seem to get it right the first time but others of us just have to pound the beat till we see the light at the end of the tunnel. I think that if it weren't for self-reflection we would all be doomed. Some people are able to do that internally and come up with their own answers and make decisions based on that and are successful. Others must seek teachers and coaches to motivate, stimulate and keep us on track. Some people are just born, I believe more mature than others and carry with them knowledge they can access from other lives they have led. I personally want to thank you for sharing your life's story with such a person as myself. Finding God in a new way and finding direction and goals for yourself, is like opening up a special Valentine's Gift. God has always shared everything he has with all of us but we turn a blind eye and think that we can do it alone. You have proved once again that we all need friends in High Places.

Love to you David on Valentine's Day

Gail

David,

Thank you so much for sending me this draft of your book. I had no idea that you were writing again during the past few years. I have watched you during your troubled times, and empathized with you, but even then you did not have the confidence in me to speak openly about your problems. I am so glad that God has come into your heart and delivered you from the spectra of "success" which you have been so at pains to project. You are more of a success with me when you are able to truthfully talk about your trials and tribulations. I too know about the "success and money" (god)-which addicted my husband throughout our married life until his death from cancer. He finally had his breakthrough just weeks before his death when he looked at all we had been through, the alcoholism, the debt, the spending, and realized that he had used his life to perpetrate a dream which sprang from his own self loathing (an abusive childhood, dyslexia and a whole long story of his own). God forgave him and welcomed him home, and he went on to meet and love those who had gone before him.

We all come into this world equipped with choice. God gives us choices, and rightly or wrongly, we use that gift to begin to understand how great and wonderful our Lord and Father is. May God's richest blessings be yours as you move on from the past "choices" which have given you the information to help others. Your trials will be useful in understanding where you fit in God's great plan. Those who have never made mistakes cannot counsel those who are in despair. I will continue to pray for you, Sue and your family as you move onward with your life.

Sharon Rounds

Hi David,

Read your book, very well done, I felt as though I was reading about myself . . . so many similarities. God is working an awesome work in me at this time also. What a blessing to know he loves us all and is no respecter of persons. I started crying when I read about your wife protecting your son, as you know I lost my son and had to go through a lot of the same things. I did walk in tough love even though it was VERY hard! Hope to talk with you and Dale soon. God Bless!

Dee

Hel-lo David Brown!

The Wealthy Farmer- an understanding of truth for me. I could feel the feelings you interpreted in and through the words you chose to express them with.

My father, as through my reaction from within while reading passed on to me the strong structure of his own father, a gift, unknown but justified by the teachings and understanding of logic throughout my upbringing. It is with you and your desire to share your story that I am able to awaken to the path that I have been traveling these past couple of years. I sought out that one person to become the teacher of Marg, giving her the answers that she felt ready to receive-feeling frustrated, blocked, stuck.... waiting for movement to carry on, something to grasp in hopes of catapulting me to the end and rejoicing in the reward of making it. You have helped me see...feel that I am to encounter many inspiring Soul's along my way, and as long as I seek, I will receive.

I want to share a quote with you that I found at my sister's scrapbooking store:

"Too often we underestimate the power of a touch, a smile
a kind word, a listening ear, an honest compliment,
or the smallest act of caring, all of which have the potential,
To turn a life around."

Your story, beautifully written as led from the magnificent creative force in this universe compassionately embraced my path in waking up to my truth. Inspiration comes from being in spirit and only from the spirit will the offering be received.

Thanks for getting it David Brown!

Smiles,
Marg

Review of The Wealthy Farmer Diary

David has an amazing drive and focus that is seen all throughout his amazing life.

Many people would have given up at any one of a number of challenges that David has faced.

David's determination and belief in the good of the word has kept him focused and centered on overcoming each challenge through God while being a good father and husband.

The result is that he follows his path through God with his family, in business and with all others whom he comes across. I know, he has touched our family and I sense the best of David is yet to come.

Joe Gorski

Hi David,

I had the opportunity to read your book. It was excellent and I related to your life's journey in a personal way. Even though my challenges were and are different from yours, I felt my journey ran parallel to yours. In the past I felt at times unworthy of my wife's love, underachieving in reaching my true potential, unproductive (lazy), unsuccessful in a financial way especially after watching the TV program: "The life of the rich and famous" and my negative perception of what others thought of me.

My wife led me to Jesus and he let me know that he was walking with me and that I was not alone.

I needed the Holy Sprit to release me from my poor self-image. As a teacher, for example, I might receive excellent feedback from all but one student. I would focus on the one person who I did not satisfy and try to figure out what I did wrong and what I should have done to make their course experience a positive one. It was always my fault.

Sorry for ranting!

God Bless you and your family for sharing your life's journey with those of us who needed to be reminded that we are not the only ones working on a less than perfect life journey. I guess that is what we take the journey for. I know that Jesus Christ and the Holy Spirit are there to listen and guide me, if I would only listen.

With your permission, may I pass your book onto someone else that God leads me to?

Once again thanks for sharing with me; all the best for your future success!

Your friend,

Doug

The Wealthy Farmer Diary

A true story about a Farmer who won't quit

The Wealthy Farmer Diary

A short story about a Farmer who won't quit

Chapter 1 – Intro-a testimony

My first book was written to help Farm &
Family Businesses perhaps see the light and
improve their lot in life. It sold 10,000 copies
and because it sold over 5,000 copies became a
best seller. For that I am thankful.

What my desire, better word, PASSION in
writing this book is that all that has happened in
our lives puts us through the refiner's fire in
order that we may share those experiences with
others so that they might be encouraged. Others
have gone through their challenges in life. I
would like as I share my true life stories and
experiences of God's never ending Grace and
Mercies, that upon reviewing not only my
challenges but also my continuing walk of faith
that if you feel so compelled to contact me and
share your experiences you too will look inside
yourself and reflect and come to truly appreciate
that there have been experiences that you too
have been through yet were kept safe and
brought out by the Grace of God. He did not
leave you but spared you so that you could live
to encourage the world around you and help
another in their walk in this life. See I

understand that through that Grace we're working through our lives. So if you would do as those did in the opening of this book in the Testimonies Section so that others might learn to succeed in-spite of.

How do we get to that point in our lives where we'd be willing to share like this, well I found that once we deal with our self esteem issues we are then in a place where we can openly and freely communicate the experiences of our lives with others for THEIR and or better YOUR OWN BENEFIT!

I am led to 'grow' beyond the simplicity of the Wealthy Farmer. Many in our great country aspire to be stewards of the land and understand biblical principles of reaping a harvest after seed has been sown.

It would be a good idea to obtain your copy of The Wealthy Farmer, as the story is about planning, and growth- the cost of producing, diversification, mentoring, and listening. The format will be the same as the Wealthy Farmer-Short chapters, Short points, Short story, Easy and Quick to read- Enjoy!

Do you know anyone diagnosed with cancer?

Do you know anyone who has faced financial ruin?

Do you know anyone affected by drugs and or alcohol addiction?

What do you think you would do?

This book took 5 years to write as it took that long for both my faith and self esteem to be raised to free me to share with you.

The book ends with a death of a precious mentor whom I loved dearly.

That death leads to everlasting life.

That person is the one that this book is dedicated to, my Father in Law:
C. William (Bill) Ferguson.

I am 47…and now 53 years old (*oops! Procrastination!)* And have a lot of life's experiences to share. This book is not about being famous, not about having all the answers, and definitely not about how to become financially wealthy. YET! (Are there self-esteem issues within those statements?) Many others who are qualified could share their knowledge. I simply offer many ideas, born of my passion for agriculture & commercial business and the North American Family and their struggles. I trust and pray that the words that I tell you through this chapter of my true-life story will both encourage and inspire you that no matter what you can overcome, through

Christ Jesus. Through my spiritual awakening my life has truly improved. And my endeavor in this is to offer you the same hope.

I thank my Lord and Savior Jesus Christ for a second and third opportunity in life to be able to share my experience; through these words, may your life be improved.

Chapter 2 - Why?

My life began on May 23, 1954 in St. Thomas, Ontario. The first two years of my life we lived in Guelph as Dad finished college at OAC (Ontario Agriculture College) University of Guelph in 1956 with a Bachelor of Science degree in Agriculture.

I grew up on a beef cash crop farm in Shedden, Ontario. My grandfather, Stewart A. Brown was the first inductee into the Ontario Agriculture Hall of Fame (in Milton, Ontario) for his contribution to the Beef Industry. If you think this book is going to be about *pride* stories or about the best farmers, think again. This is a story about humility, love, common sense and commitment to agriculture. Agriculture is a way of life for many here and many farm families are really hurting right now.

In a future book I will address the needs of progressive farmers and answer the questions pertaining to "how do I?" that were omitted from the first book. You may use the first book, "The Wealthy Farmer," as a foundation of my desire or passion to help people overcome.

The next section of this book is difficult for me to write, as I must relive a very traumatic time in my life. A time where I needed to make some decisions on which road to take for the rest of my life in order to really live. It is not intended for pity or sympathy.

What happened?

It was prior to Christmas 2001 when I began to experience a great level of discomfort in the area of the male genitalia. I had gone to my doctor and after an examination sent me for an ultrasound of my testicles which revealed nothing. I then requested a blood test for the detection of prostate cancer. The results of that test would change my life forever.

Chapter 3 - Results

The results of a normal PSA (prostate specific antigen) test ranges between 1-4.
Mine came back 23½. Something was going on that wasn't good in my body.
I was sent to a new Urologist who discovered a lump on my prostate gland and sent me for CT scans and X-rays on my kidneys. All came back negative. Thanks be- to God!
However his remarks before and after the test results were less than encouraging. In essence, if I had stayed, his words would have killed me. See I now understand that the power one uses or yields with their tongue through their words if you allow yourself to receive them into your spirit can be detrimental to your health. Your emotions are tied up with your physical, look at all the high blood pressure statistics, most due to stress and poor diet and lack of exercise, along with many of the cancers too. Now if you believe what is said to or about you the information can deceive your spirit. You know like when a judge tells the jury to strike that from the record, or disregard that last statement, as though they didn't hear it. Now you know regardless to what the judge says, the attorney which used that tactic/trick knows the power of suggestion, once heard it's imbedded. The same goes with the aforementioned from what doctors tell you regarding their diagnosis, even though correct in their assessment, it doesn't mean that

it ends with their words. I have, however since learned to forgive him for the untrue facts he shared and the truth he did not yet know. *"For Greater is He who is in me than he who is in this world."* That is my truth.

I am going to say something right now that will help ANYONE currently going through a difficult situation, especially medical. This is not meant to criticize or put down the medical profession at all. It is being said to help those diagnosed with a potentially serious or perhaps terminal illness, in the opinion of a medical professional.

Here it is:

It is most unhealthy to allow yourself to be put in a position where a doctor, or any professional and or someone you know and trust on a personal level for that matter to take authority over your life with their words. There is only one authority over all of life and that is God and His Word, and in it is the Power of Life. A Word from God our Almighty Creator, the Designer of our bodies, the *"One who knew you before you were formed"(Jeremiah 1:5, Isaiah 44:24-27)* can do some things mighty special. Our God has the ability to change a reality that seems dim, and why, because we have faith in His Word, and your faith according to Hebrews 11:23-25 in the Bible only need be *"the size of a mustard seed"* to move your mountain, your issue- whatever that may be. Let no man take that trust of our Heavenly Father away from you- no man, for in Him is the avenue of life forever in this life and the hereafter!

If you hear this or realize this, it could save your life as it did mine. Today I am a healed man of God being positioned and trained as an evangelist for Him.

I was fortunate to have been able to see one of the finest Urologists in the country, Dr. John Valleley and his assistant Leslie Rogers. His kind words spoken to a person, not a disease, began a healing process in me, which manifests daily through increased faith. His words were encouragement and developed hope and faith. They didn't destroy hope and faith. They gave the gift of hope and faith. This is very important.

One of the wisest gestures you can make for yourself in this life is to always surround yourself with positive, helpful faith-filled people. Psalm 1:1-3 reminds us that we are blessed when we do not walk in the counsel of the ungodly and when we are not influenced by and associate with sinful people. This has changed my life, and because I've chosen to surround myself with likeminded individuals I get the fulfillment of the passage in v.3 of Psalm

1, *"Like a tree planted by streams of water that gives its own fruit in its season."*

The first portions of this book are a mini autobiography to help others see the balance needed in life.

Chapter 4 - What did I do?

I obtained a second opinion. I listened to my sister, Linda whom I love dearly, who confessed with her mouth "I would not die!" as our earthly father did from prostate cancer. She led me to a church called Word of Faith International Christian Center. Praise God! I got into agreement with her about living vs. dying as well as seeking and finding healing for my 'earth suit', our body. This encounter and the decision to attend another Church saved my life here on earth.

I would say to anyone reading this book (without sounding critical) that if you are "uncomfortable" with your Church and find yourself hungry for more of God and His Word, allow God to move you to a place where you are growing in your faith daily.
Pray about this huge decision and let God lead you to another level of faith. This is much more

positive than remaining in a place where you feel unchallenged to change.

Currently, for the carnal skeptics in the flesh, my PSA reading is now 0.28.
The Doctors call it "near perfect". It IS perfect because it is God's work!

As I write now, 5-years later, the PSA reading is 0.07. Had I been diagnosed one year later I would have been listening to a "terminal diagnosis!" Don't trust man to keep you healthy! Trust God to give you good common sense in looking after your body with healthy foods, exercise and equally as these two your emotional well being, your thought life, as mentioned they can dictate many unfavorable results.

I sit here in the park and listen to the thunder roll! I love the storm and any kind of weather!

Distant thunder rolls announcing an impending storm while my eyes are drawn to the canvas of Gods artistic expression as I sit here, pen to paper, in this park. My senses are filled with such indescribable beauty, the magnitude of which reaches into the deepest depths of my soul and wakens a spiritual understanding, a profound realization and appreciation for what God so freely gives us and which we so carelessly cast aside as 'just the weather'. I love all kinds of weather. It humbles me and makes me appreciate Him and life more.

With this in mind I realize that I'm truly blessed for I have a precious wife, Susan of 31 years on Sept, 18 /07. I am also blessed with three children: Jesse 28, Dustin 24, and Cali 19.

Chapter 5 - Reflections

I'd like to say that I relate to readers who, have experienced various tests and trials and, by God's grace, have overcome; as a result they became victorious and developed patience, knowledge of life and grew in love and understanding. They, as did I grew to trust God's view of their lives and appreciated this life and other human beings even more. Recently I watched the movies "Facing The Giants" and "Conversations with God" that really illustrate this point.

The first Blessing was December 1977, Susan and I had been married a little over a year. We were returning from a company Christmas party. I had been drinking and was very tired. I was driving a new 1976 Monte Carlo and was speeding. Then suddenly we came upon a curve in the road, and I'd fallen asleep behind the wheel. Susan quickly grabbed the wheel but the car went into a sideways skid into a lane way, then into a deep ditch, flipping over several times before landing in the ditch.

I couldn't believe that I nearly killed the most beautiful woman I had admired and longed to go out with since high school. She was so popular in high school while I was not.

Susan's back was broken as was my jaw. I almost killed the most precious person in my life. The Lord spared us as He did before. (My spirit confirms this as I write) We are so blessed. Our God is a good and Mighty God.

The car finally stopped falling, and flipping and came to rest upside down on its roof, still running and now leaking gas. With a broken back Susan was still able to climb out of the car and while fearing an explosion any second, came back through the back window of the car to drag me out she was awesome! She was unaware that she had two crushed vertebrae in her lower back. It's a miracle she wasn't paralyzed. Our car didn't explode, thank God. But she didn't know that at the time. Can you imagine the excruciating pain she must have been in, she risked her life for mine. God I Love that woman, I love her! I have tears welling up in my eyes as I write this. A person who loves you as much as she loves me comes about once in a lifetime and often never for many. I am truly blessed.

Susan's back healed and so did my jaw. She was told she would never have children after that because her pelvic bone had shifted and she would be unable to deliver a child. Well, you already know that we have been blessed with three children. They are all healthy, outgoing, active, intelligent, and good looking. (Thank you Lord!)

I made the mistake in the first book of talking about things I knew little about (financial management.) A subject I do know a lot about is life!

The second Blessing occurred, when I was 36, during a footrace.

By the way, I'm not sharing these accounts of my life looking for pity or anything like it. I share because I sincerely love you (The God kind of Love-Agape', Greek for enduring, because it never fails, as the Word of God commands us as the second commandment "Love your neighbor as yourself") well I love me, so I love you too, and want so much for you to be encouraged in some small way from your experience of reading this book. I want you to benefit from God's blessings as I have.

It was a very hot early August morning in 1990. I had written my final C.M.A.

(Certified Management Accounting Exam) and passed after 12 years of correspondence courses (That's another story). I was training to get in shape for OLD TIMERS HOCKEY (the over 35 league) in St. Thomas, Ontario. I decided I needed "wind" and "better wheels" for legs. As I am a competitor, I really needed to be in better shape if you know what I mean. So I began, for the first time in my life to jog- Whoo! This was no joke it was a feat! I began at 1 km, 2 km, up and up, and as I stretched my goals, I went further and further weekly. By working hard I got all the way up to 14 km all in a period of 4 months. I dropped about 15 lbs along the way.

Well, to cap off my new found pastime of getting in shape by running I entered a 12 km race from St. Thomas to Port Stanley, Ontario Canada, a journey said to be downhill heading due south to Lake Erie. The week before the 12 km race I ran the course in 60 minutes with my son Jesse was 11 years old then. He rode his bike and carried my water for me. Everything went AOK.

Race day came. It was a clear, blue sky and extremely hot. We were bussed from the Port Stanley Arena and the much anticipated race had arrived it had about 150 competitors. I checked beforehand for water "stops" along the way. The organizers assured us, I didn't have to take water for the race. There were supposedly at least 6 water stations along the route.

Off I went at a quick pace, keeping right up with some long time joggers from the local jogging club, "The Jumbo Striders". I was running along side a High School teacher from my era, and determined to keep him beside me. We approached the 3 km mark and I grabbed water. At 5 km, 7 km, 9 km, no water was available. The water stations weren't prepared for the traffic that occurred.

It became truly all "downhill" for me. They ran out of water at every km from then on until I collapsed at 10.4 km from severe heat stroke and heat exhaustion. My family has just driven by waving at me (with plenty of water in the vehicle). After I fell, a well-meaning lady came out of her house and poured cold water on me in an attempt to cool me down, She did it from a kind heart. My body went into a state of shock I was then picked up by an ambulance.

The ambulance Attendants shoved oxygen up to my face to bring me around somewhat and then they decided to transfer me to another ambulance and take me to the hospital, which was 12 km away. This ambulance took me to the finish line. (Unofficially I finished the race). While lying in the second ambulance I spoke to God. I was in fear. I was experiencing death. Later I was told that my blood was so hot it was picking up enzymes in my leg muscles. I was terrified to think that I would die at the age of 36 years of age.

Then I 'came' to my senses and thanked God that Susan, Jesse and Dustin and Cali were okay and it was me that was dying and not them, I was okay with that thought, you know being the protective husband and father. In surrendering to God, my fear turned to complete peace. No I did not see anybody or visit another place. But I knew I was away from this earth for a short time. During that experience unbeknown to me, for what really do we base our lives on, isn't it the now, and the reflections of yesterdays past. I could have spent eternity in hell and just feel like we have no clue; well I had no clue then, but Glory to God for favor and knowing my future, for I don't know my future but He does. I tell you death was real to me, I said: "Good-bye, I love you" to Susan because at that time I felt it was time for me to die so I thought, but God had other plans for me- Grace! I was not yet born again. (A new person in Christ, or better yet Christ dwelling within me by my willingness to yield my life over to Him as my Lord and Savior.)

I left my body for a time. I was not yet born again. I could have spent an eternity in Hell Now I know God's grace.

The second ambulance took me to the emergency department of the hospital. My vital signs disappeared for a short time. All I remember was 'coming to' looking at the fluorescent lights of the emergency ward, Susan at my side, and thanking God.

Crying uncontrollably and confessing to Susan I said, "I think God wants me to become a minister" I didn't realize that was a self-fulfilling prophecy, as I would someday become a minister, I am studying to become one now.

I experienced more of God's grace in February of 2002.

As I share this, I don't want anyone who reads this book to look at it as a religious story. I have been led these past years by God and have done His will and have been touched by His love every time. Working for God is awesome and liberating!

The faith building exercise I have grown through in past months has been incredible! I chose to give my circumstances, diagnosis, fears, stress, mortality and disease to God. He IS in control. But I have learned we have to be receivers of His Word if we plan to benefit from His protection, healing and salvation.

Yes, we do have a part to play; we must take in God's word and feed on and from Him daily through word study and our only way to speak with Him through prayer. God has provided us with various ways to get that food, be it: The Churches, Internet, TV-Cable programs, cassettes and CDs, they all have teachings based on God's Word. As explained and expanded upon by one of God's Ministerial Warriors, Dr. Kenneth E. Hagin, who was instructed by God to "teach my people faith". Since then my faith has been built up tremendously and I trust the One who sees my future, I Love my Heavenly Father.

Chapter 6 – The Truth

I grew up on a Beef Cash Crop Farm near Shedden, Ontario. Growing up I always admired my cigar smoking Grandfather who was very successful in the farming business and full of wisdom and quite knowledgeable about business in general. He appeared to be all about business and money. But I learned later he really loved people for was also about helping them, primarily by lending or giving them money. He had it to give. My Grandfather helped his brothers obtain educations at auctioneering and medical school. He was a giver. He was a good man. But he expected a lot from his children and grandchildren. He was inducted into the Ontario Agriculture Hall of Fame in Milton, Ontario. I was and am proud of my grandfather and his legacy. I wanted so much to live my life like my grandfather lived his. As I write these words tears well up in my eyes. I have not lived up to my grandfather's expectations for my life. I have not become, as yet, successful in business or in finances. I write these words as a reflection of the way I used to think. I will reveal how I changed my thinking in the chapter called "Miracles and Westover". My self-esteem was low because I hadn't yet lived up to the perceived expectations of my Grandfather & Father, both of whom have been laid to rest years ago.

My Grandfather, full of knowledge passed along one piece of wisdom to me as a 6 year old boy, that wisdom "save every penny"! My response was one of rejection and disappointment as a little boy because that meant I would no longer be able to go to the corner store and buy a chocolate bar for myself. I am not blaming my Grandfather for any personal disappointments (only failure if nothing learned). I have learned a great deal to this point, "I/you don't have to live up to anyone else's expectations but your own!"

My father was a good man. When he died of cancer 9 years ago it hurt me. My father had a record attendance at the funeral home. Many people loved my father. He had many friends. However he died without health or money. He did however die while being loved by many. That was a victory!

My father and I had listened, but not heeded, my grandfather's admonition on saving. I watched my father spend and borrow and complain over the years about the poor results from the farm. It didn't have a chance because those (my father and relatives), who were farming the land didn't earn the right to farm it. Much of it was inherited from my grandfather; so many times that which is given can be so unappreciated. I saw my father spend and borrow, spend and borrow. And I didn't learn anything either, I duplicated my father, I have led a life spending and borrowing. I have lived most of my life in financial bondage.

Let me stop right here. If anyone, family or friend or any reader is assuming that the reason for this chapter is to lay blame for the author's lack of success to this point, they are grossly mistaken. I write as it was and is- *The Truth*. This is how I perceive why I am where I am. It is not a put down. I still love and respect all that my grandfather and father did for me big time. But I am attempting to unlock the doors for many a reader by putting my thoughts and my perspectives on paper so that perhaps the truth from my terrible bondage of a life of debt may begin to open your eyes and cast a light upon a great darkness, and yield an awesome revelation towards freedom.

"You will know the truth and the truth shall set you free!" (John 8:32)
We seldom look for answers and solutions to life's problems when the sailing is smooth. They are found when looking up from the deepest parts of the valleys we go through. We also learn the most when we fall. Many don't get back up. But with God's help, and His Word, I did! You can too! Yes, you can!

Chapter 7 - Life's Meaning

Growing up on the farm I thought that by the time I hit 50 years of age, with growth and maturity, I would own a few farms, I'd be happily married with well-adjusted children who all excelled at school. I envisioned being a multi-millionaire semi retired with all the money and all the answers as well. Well I didn't and am not-yet. In the previous chapter, I revealed my Achilles heel throughout my life thus far. The love of money and what it would buy and the good feeling having plenty would bring. What I learned from growing up through observation of my family as mentioned in previous chapters was to buy what I (wanted) when I thought I needed it. I had followed the pattern I grew up with. If you need (or want) something, don't wait, buy it now and pay for it later, without savings and satisfy your desire to possess material objects even though after, you felt shame and guilt.

You know I remember when I had written the first book in this series, and Dupont Canada purchased 4,000 copies and used them for a new product launch out in Western Canada. A lady from out west wrote me and accused my family of being simple…based on that book she said the format used was too simple in dialogue/story format. She was right. We were. We are. Some of us "missed it". I have up to this point. I missed it BIGTIME! I thank God for honest straight shooting people like her.

You know when I wrote that book as with this one the message behind the stories were intended for some average and ordinary folks who can relate to dealing with challenges like what I dealt with and am continuing to deal with. More importantly are like myself looking for some answers in how to cope with those challenges. It's for you, it's for me, and yes it's pretty simple; but we touched a nerve because Dupont Canada purchased 4,000 copies, that says a lot.

I have, at this time in my life, completed an O.A.C, (Ontario Agriculture College Diploma program). I have, through the love and support of my family, completed 12 grueling years of study while working full time earning a living.

In addition, I have earned 23 University equivalent courses in order to be designated as a Certified Management Accountant (CMA). I have also written a book called The Wealthy Farmer, which is a best seller in Canada. (Sales over 5,000 copies) I have been on TV, Radio and have done public speaking, but I hadn't learned much about who I was until recent years.

I have been back in the classroom learning how the market place deals with mature or 'seasoned' workers. I am no longer self-employed. And yes, I have been in a cashless situation. Not a good place to be at the age of 50. How did it happen? Good business model. Bad timing. Not identifying, dealing with or hiring those who would have complemented my weaknesses. I learned I don't have to know how to be a mechanic but I 'd better know how to hire one who's good, very good at what he does to keep my business running smoothly and efficiently in that area. What I found is that I was really ignorant to what it really means to run a business, they call it "details", and sharing job tasks, I'm still learning; it's a growing process, I know that now.

Because of what I didn't fully appreciate from behind the counter or I should say on the other side of the counter, my customer service suffered. Attention to detail I guess the small significant stuff just wasn't fully understood.

Because I was getting more and more frustrated my family life suffered big-time, as a result I ended up with a serious illness diagnosis. Cash expenses exceeded cash flow. Our marketing programs targeted only farmers with High debt, Mad Cow, Avian Flu, Walkerton Water and personal money management yet we were getting caught between clients and their accountants as active contract controllers and everyone was on a different page. All I wanted was the best for the farmer and small business owner.

First a solo corporate initiative and then a partnership initiative failed to succeed. That business was a tremendous teacher but wasn't meant to be. After that I needed some mature counseling sessions.

I am 53 years old now. Two years ago I attended a session to learn about how I 'fit' into the work force or market place.

How DO we fit? Throughout my life I have devoted a great deal of my time to the accounting profession, it's responsibilities, guidelines, I fought the details, and the dry and generally rigid, inflexible structure that goes with it.

At one point while writing I have completed two courses on 'fitting in' as a 'mature' or seasoned worker in the marketplace. The other was a testing utilizing various colors from a color chart or wheel defining who you are and how your characteristics really fit into the work marketplace.

To explain, there are four colors, which represent character traits or personalities. Orange is outgoing, blue is emotional, green is analytical, and gold is organized. A typical accountant is dominant gold with green as a second color, or personality. I tested as orange with blue as a second color. I discovered that I am all about People, Sales, and Marketing. In fact, the subsequent tests reflected, for example that I would become a Religious Leader, and/or Insurance salesman. These are things I didn't know intellectually but "knew" in my heart. I believed the world had suppressed my growth as a businessman. Then came an evolution to sales and marketing, or better yet, manifestations as a 'salesman' I realized then that had been denying, suppressing and even avoiding up to two years ago, this new me! The Revelation that came from these programs was supplying this

I wear a ring with the letters CMA (Certified Management Accountant) on it. I have a plaque on my wall that says that I have a professional accounting designation, but I am no longer an accountant at heart. I have the experience but not the desire any longer. I had changed for a greater purpose. It was being revealed to me. When the student is ready…the teacher will appear. The teacher was right in front of me. Calling me to change to serve and sell and to later become a humble, obedient servant and love and help His people.

I am, as stated earlier, all about helping people through ministry, sales and marketing.

What a tragedy for the new me, and my life if I had kept applying for bookkeeping accounting or controller type roles. That's not what I am cut out for or would be happy doing. The right thing for me is to 'venture' out into a sales and marketing role.

At the time of writing this chapter, I was training to "sell a service" to the public. A Financial Service, from what I understood, to farmers and small business owners.

Twice in my life I have found it a joy to get up and go to work. The first time was when I trained to become a credit manager and now. I liked credit because it was connected to Sales and Service!

My attempt at being an entrepreneur did not succeed because I did not have structured Green and Gold aptitude to support what I was attempting to do. I have come to realize that the main reason I obtained an accounting designation was because:

a- I wanted to prove (to the world) that I was smart and
b- I was seeking the APPROVAL of my father-in-law.

Was it something I wanted to do? NO! Was it something I needed to do to please others and build self-esteem? Well-Yes. I became an accountant for all the wrong reasons!!!
I was attempting to live up to others expectations for my life! Now I understand why.

Chapter 8 - Miracles and Westover

Westover is a place where good people with bad habits such as drug addiction and alcoholism go to 'clean up and step up into their lives through a 12-step program. The three- week program has a high success ratio and is one of the best in the country. It has a 7-day family program for those directly affected by drugs or alcohol; I attended the latter, my son attended the former.

The hell on earth that my family lived in and around through my sons' cocaine addiction for two-years, had a profound and negative effect on our family, I soon discovered. But during the family program I discovered many things that I did not know about myself. The silver lining surrounding the cloud of cocaine addiction was what David Brown would discover about himself. A precious gift was about to present itself after I had totally yielded to humility.

I didn't like myself. I didn't love myself. I was attempting to live up to my Grandfather and Fathers expectations for my life, of which both have sense passed on- one for decades now. What an utterly futile and self-defeating mindset for my life.

I also had to deal with debt and grief in dealing with money matters. I was taught that money; position, power and self-esteem were related. I was very wrong.

During my stay at Westover, initially, there was a get acquainted time. There were both women and men in our group. It was determined by all, at the outset, that I was indeed the winner of any award given for being the angriest person in the group. This came as a result of watching, helplessly, my wife enable my son during a two-year period and not being permitted to discipline or be a father to a son in trouble as my wife protected him in every way possible; to the extent of helping him out of problems, big problems financially.

I was a psychological and emotional mess when I entered Westover. I couldn't think straight. The program began to work on building my self worth and esteem and taught me how to begin to care for and look after David again. David was beginning to like himself.

Chapter 9 - Faith

I am now, at the time of writing this chapter, 50 years of age. I have lived most of my life in fear and torment. Westover diagnosed me as having Post Traumatic Stress Disorder. Even though my blood pressure was elevated due to contributing circumstances I'm sure, however the flip side in the positive was my cancer diagnosis was healed. Thank God. All at once I felt a peace, a tremendous peace that I did not die of cancer as so many other friends and family have gone before me. Psalm 91 comes to mind: ***"1,000 shall fall at my side and 10,000 at my right hand but it shall not come near me"***. I give God the Glory for the air that I breathe, for I live!

I would always research their death and find a common denominator. That common denominator was this: Each and every one either received bad news about being terminally ill, but instead of putting God's Word first, as their final authority, they made the doctor their final authority. They listened to the diagnosis given and from that point on prepared not to live, but to die. They do exactly that. The other thought present is to expect the worst. (At this point the book of Job comes to mind.) They speak and act and receive and believe that something bad will happen to them and it does, remarkably, 100% of the time. There is a movie that has been produced called "The Secret". It supports this thought. "The Law of attraction." With the emphasis being on "what the mind can conceive the heart will achieve!" Or in the physiological affecting you internally because you are telling your brain or overwriting an outward spoken directive with your internal command, that's awesome, and that's the power of God, He placed all this wonder within us if we would only tap into it.

What was different with my case? I listened to the Doctors and rejected their bad news.
I expected to live, to have victory over disease, and not doubt God's grace, love, mercy and His healing power. It's that simple. God wants us to believe, receive and speak with confidence His Word over our lives. What many do is speak out the problem over their lives and not God's Word. These are end times. I am not an end-time naysayer; I do however believe that if there was ever a time for miracles it is NOW!

Chapter 10 - Building Self Esteem

Throughout my life, because of my upbringing, I expected to keep the silver spoon in my mouth and succeed because of my father and grandfather's success. I hadn't planned on dropping the spoon in my own lifetime. Losing the spoon frequently had become my reality, but to lose it for good- is was what ultimately had happened. The spoon is a representation of money, (the obsessed love and desire of it). I focused on the money instead of the people. I focused on the wrong thing. In 1 Timothy 6:10 it states: *"The LOVE of money is the root of all evil."* Not MONEY- The LOVE of it!

I loved the silver spoon; it represented pride, ego, family, and name. What it should 'look like' to the rest of the world. It almost destroyed my life. Living up to the terms of what I thought success was and looked like. That was a term (silver-spoon) that a dear counselor Tammy Willert at the Cancer Clinic in London Ontario coined. What it looked like from the road. The Brown Family had to look good from the road! Although we were no different or better than anyone else! I am who I am now! Not my father's son or grandfather's grandson. I am proud of what they accomplished in their lives, they did a great deal of good for others as we experienced at Dad's funeral. David is living up to David's expectation for his life now. I am quickly giving up on what the world thinks of or about me. I am focused on pleasing God with my faith and selflessly serving others.

At the time of final edits I can honestly say I no longer care about what my family members thinks about me. That is liberating! I cast that care onto the Lord for good. I still love them and forgive them regardless of their need to judge others. It isn't them, it's the enemy on them; we are doing the best we can. Our best is getting better because of faith. *(Thank you Tammy for the phrases: "What it looks like from the road" and "Doing the best we can every day.")*

So I say, Greater is He who is in me than he who is in this world!

My self-esteem suffered as I focused materially during my life instead of walking in Love as Jesus instructed us to do. What I thought esteemed me of value was the beginning of my sufferings, now I have the One Who is the Beginning of Value!

My "emotional tank" was empty and if you don't love yourself you cannot and will not love others. Others will pick up on this and you will not and cannot connect with them. Love is the key that unlocks many a heart, many a door. In Matthew 7:7 we are told: *"Seek and you will find, ask and you will receive, knock and the door will be opened to you."* We need to speak out God's Word of Faith and not fear, doubt or be in unbelief.

Personal faults need to be corrected, no ... forgiven by self, to truly live life.

The biggest challenge I have had in my life is keeping focused and on track on the most important tasks and not getting bogged down in unnecessary detail. Details are important but too many can be distractions.

I have found for me if you get buried in too much activity, i.e.; the paper work, people pleasing, internet, cell phones, TV and all the other automated gadgets in our lives, we can get cluttered in our minds and it's so easy in our society today not to prioritize. With all the 'too much' that we have, we don't realize that it can actually be interference in our lives against what matters most. We all need to simplify our lives. I believe instead that we need to spend more time listening to the still small voice inside of every believer instead of drowning Him out. When John 10:10 says: ***"The enemy comes to kill, steal, and destroy."*** One of the things he's trying to steal is our time and our attention away from God.

Early every morning I meditate and pray in spite of (at one time) creditor calls, demands on my time and focusing on my low bank account as a result of all of the foolish and impulsive personal financial decisions 'yours truly' has made. This 15-20 minute prayer time centers me for the day. I receive a fresh insight for each day in spite of the bills or stresses, family issues, and goals to be achieved. Demands come from everywhere... demands on our time, energy and financial resources. One cannot possibly hear what one needs to hear from the Holy Spirit and receive the Word of God if one is in strife, and turmoil, or as mentioned so much clutter mentally that you can't even focus, let alone hear God.

Let's discuss strife, unrest and stress for a moment. On a previous weekend almost two years ago I attended Word of Faith International Christian Center in Southfield, Michigan (the church I currently attend) and heard a Bible discourse given by a Pastor Rick Renner. Dr. Renner and his wife are starting up Churches all over the former Soviet Union Praise God! He spoke of the story of The Apostle Paul. Many of you reading this book will relate to this story and teaching.

The story begins in Acts, chapter 9, where Saul of Tarsus (who was later named Paul) stopped on the way to Damascus to persecute Christians after Christ was crucified.
He eventually became born again responding to Jesus' question *"Saul, Saul, why do you persecute me?"*

As a result of his experience on the road to Damascus, Paul became temporarily blind.
For 3 days Paul was without food or water, and spent that time in prayer. During this time, God

gave Saul a vision of the forthcoming healing. This temporary blindness was not Jesus inflicting disease - this was Jesus/God the Father getting Paul to be STILL in order to prepare him for Ministry.

Once Paul's sight was restored at the hand of Ananias, he was baptized and straightway preached Christ in the Synagogues, and that He is the Son of God and that God had resurrected Jesus now the only true way to approach God the Father (Acts 9:20). The Lord told Ananias that Paul (Acts 9:15) *"is a chosen vessel unto me, to bear my name before the Gentiles, and kings, and the children of Israel"*.
Subsequently Paul was persecuted in several ways (The reason why is outlined in Acts 9:16 and the full litany is outlined in 2 Corinthians 11:23).

He encountered strife, stress, trouble, disaster, and problems of all kinds. A thorn in the flesh kept him humble. Through it all he learned to trust God and experience His grace.
2 Corinthians 12:7 in the NIV version of the Bible, shows clearly that Paul's thorn was not a disease. This *"thorn"* was a messenger from Satan; 2 Timothy 3:10-11 states: *"The Lord rescued me (Paul) from ALL of them (sufferings) including his thorn."* (See 2 Corinthians 12:9-10) Can this be said of you, dear Reader? When difficult circumstances come knocking on your door, allow God to

answer the door for you. It's time to reflect and meditate on God's Word and ask for guidance.

Take a look, for example at Psalm 61:2, *"From the end of the earth I will cry to you, when my heart is overwhelmed; lead me to the rock that is higher than I."* And Psalm 27:5 reads… *"For in the time of trouble He shall hide me in His pavilion; in the secret place of His tabernacle He shall hide me; He shall set me high upon a rock."*

When you are at your lowest, allow God to pick you up out of your circumstances. Friend, when He places you on a rock higher than yourself, your vantage point changes, and so does the perception of what you are experiencing.

It was through utilizing this aspect of God's Grace, His Word, and His loving kindness for me as one of His sons that I was able to change my perspective on my life and begin the long road of recovery.

Chapter 11 - Stresses: The Absence of Trust & Faith In God

Stress, or I should say the ability to feel pressure prompts us to do, or to make change, to alert us that something is or may be wrong. The stress hormone is a physiological alarm aspect of being human. How we deal with that alarm shaped in the form of pressure or intense alertness is an entirely different matter, how we see the situations or occurrences happening can prove fatal to us physically if not addressed properly. We need to look at this subject for a minute or two.

For over 30 years it has been an issue for me. Stress combined with negative thinking, shame and guilt, have held me back from living a truly successful and abundant life as set out in John 10:10. What we do in our life depends on our thinking. We are what our thoughts tell us we are. *"For as a man thinketh in his heart, so is he!"* (Proverbs 23:7) Let me ask you…Is Christ your treasure?

Let's not kid ourselves if we (I) have made some mistakes financially by taking on too much debt, it becomes a trap. That trap, with the help of shame and guilt, holds you down and doesn't let you truly live a life of joy.

Debt. More Debt. Debt plus Interest, Extended terms... Pay later... 0- Down ... Refinance... More credit... Doesn't matter about your credit.

Credit is a privilege, not a right. When attempting to provide a service to farmers to enable them to know their cost of production prior to planting or seeding and subsequent harvest, I used the availability of loans/credit through increasing credit card debt. DUMB. You see I am not perfect either. That was certainly not good advice to anyone or myself. See in yesteryear I was WORSE than you. What did I do later? I stopped using a credit card for anything. I lost my privilege, and rightfully so.

The World does not owe me anything. The World's system (that aspect which is controlled by Satan) is waiting to suck you in (as it did me), beat you up and spit you out, as it tried to do to me.

We must not allow sophisticated marketing and 'in-your-face' demands to spend reckless and thoughtlessly- suck us in. We don't need it now. We need to see if we can pay cash for those items first thereby putting a 'monkey wrench' in our need for immediate gratification which in many instances proves to become a delayed and or postponed anxiousness setting you and I up for failure. (See James 4:1-3)

Discipline with paying off a credit card account monthly is what is needed. Still working on that one. I'm almost there.

Chapter 12 - Anger

I recently attended a Farm Show as an exhibitor. You might remember my "colors" have "changed". Right- Remember?

I am no longer into details, paperwork and the little things. I am into people, helping to encourage, raising self-esteem so that others may go out and serve our Heavenly Father. The purpose is to win souls for Christ, on the premise, *"to keep seeking first the kingdom of God and all other things will be added to you."* (Matthew 6:33)

I once did some tax work for a gentleman's brother who was upset over what he perceived to be my error; he was wrong. As a result he expressed his feelings of anger in a very hostile manner. To the best of my knowledge, the error had occurred as a result of inadequate information being included at the time of filing. One can only work with what one has been presented to work with. However, he was raising his voice and yelling at me in a crowd of more than 100 people. At the time I was thinking about the chastisement of Jesus by Pilate where Jesus said nothing.

He yelled… I listened. Some of what he said was true, most wasn't. He was upset so I continued to listen. There were other things happening in his life that were upsetting to him and all of it was coming out as blame on me. I applied, *"Love Thy Neighbor As Thy self."* And I loved him unconditionally using the God kind of Agape (Greek root) Love. Was that easy, no but it was a choice, something I now understand we have an option to do. But to love is a command from God, we do it when we probably wouldn't want to, I'm sure for the same reasons we'd want God to Love us when we know we don't deserve it but He gives anyway, because He knows we need it, to move on and make progress in our lives. This man's wife was a cancer survivor. His brother had died of cancer.   He had issues behind his feelings that weren't all rooted in the current circumstances.   I am beginning to see bad behavior separate from the good person. It helps me. Bad behavior and bad attitude steal one's joy.

I listened. When asked to respond I said 'no'. All that I was lead to say was, "you have no idea what I have been through." That "what" was a cancer diagnosis of my own and a death sentence, according to the urologist, that had "wrote me off" three years earlier.

(The time of the tax work) At that time I wasn't doing well. I had cried and not slept for two weeks until faith took hold and the Lord sent me my dear sister Linda to speak words of encouragement over my life. The House had been sold two months earlier after 22 years. My 21-year-old son was put out of the house. All of my financial dreams and allusions almost had me declare personal and corporate bankruptcy. Why? Because I had invested almost all I had into helping primarily farmers like the gentleman who stood in front of me berating me with a tongue tainted with evil words. Not him. It was the enemy.

How's that for irony. I changed. The market place didn't. That gentleman hadn't yet. I have prayed for him and I know my Heavenly Father will soften his heart. Forgive the person and forget the sin. Like how our Father does in meting out Mercies and Grace to and on us.

I learned at Westover that it doesn't matter what people think of me. It used to. It matters more to me what people think of themselves verses what they think of me. People with low self-esteem will yell and scream at you, I know, I used to do it (and still do I really don't mean to) at times at my wife and children. Some Christian Father and husband eh? I have a long way to go.

Chapter 13 - Addiction

Is farming an addiction? I say yes. Many would disagree. Many would agree.

It's word play. Planting/seeding has been in high gear now for a few weeks at the time of writing this chapter. There is nothing more exciting to a farm boy than to drive by a field being marked off for seed by its owner/renter. When I wrote the first book, its primary purpose was to help farmers determine their cost of production. Only after considering the costs for seeding and how that relates to the eventual harvest and whether or not the weatherman had been good to them. I believe for many they would not know what to do if they didn't have a tractor to operate in the field they work. If this sounds too simplistic…good! I am making a simple point. (I was accused by a western grain farmer in my first book of being too SIMPLE and that basically my ancestors must have been 'simple' as well). We are! Never judge a book by its cover or chapters unless you really know the author! It was an attempt at a put down. It didn't work. I am beyond all insults and criticisms, as this book is an act of love not one of money, self-interest, selfishness or fame seeking. I prayed for that lady. Better yet, I have forgiven that lady if she meant harm. I believe her to be, as mentioned earlier, a straight shooter.

The bottom line is that farming has become more complicated and if the simplicity of farming is gone, and an addiction to farm is overriding all sound decision making processes, then the farmer and his farm assets will be at risk as well.

When my son Dustin "entertained" drugs such as cocaine to help him "face life", the drugs took over his life. He was no longer functioning as a healthy young man making rational decisions in the world.

No, I am not comparing farmers to drug addicts. Am I? Maybe I am. Addictions are the bi-product of affliction within one's own spirit; you know what I mentioned earlier about the low self-esteem. Basically a poor self-image based upon our surrounding influences and our personal view of ourselves can project unrealistic expectations of us in general. I'm finding that when we don't either live up to those expectations or get rid of them altogether we will get addicted to something, we shouldn't but we do.

One who has become addicted to farming regardless to consistent struggles at the threat of loss of all that we value has placed their drug of choice as their land. If they are able to navigate danger, rules, regulation, detail, paperwork, environmental and government guidelines and know that they can create a reasonably profitable situation. GREAT! Their costs are lower than their input 'THEN' they should proceed! If, however, they are caught in a cycle with no plan and no vision that would show a profit, they should STOP FARMING!!!

My desire to help farmers was a REAL Life ADDICTION PROCESS!

Yours truly had put his heart, soul and time into a business, a farmer related self-help book and much of his, and others money into an attempt (an addiction I had) to help farmers understand and benefit by first knowing their cost of production. 10% of those I spoke to and worked with were listening and applying their knowledge to know their accounting and numbers to plan and profit better. 90% of the rest said they could listen for a bit and some even tried to change, but eventually went back to their OLD WAYS!

I invested 5 years of my life into a passion to help farmers better utilize the cost of production and it almost bankrupted me. That was an addiction. That was foolish.
I am not a foolish man. That activity was. I am 51 years of age in a few weeks at the time of writing this chapter. I live in a 2-bedroom apartment with my wife and daughter.
The creditors are calling. The debt has to be paid. I have a proposal in place to pay off all of my creditors.

That my friend, farmer, is the end result of an addictive 'at all cost' attitude. I don't have the right to keep borrowing money to do what I 'love" at the expense of those I love. Friend, neither do you!

This chapter is a wake up call. A call to positive action and a call for some of you to begin changing the way you think; change your mind and your farming and business strategies, once and for all!

I recently met a young farmer, who is the son of a dear friends friend, who decided to stop doing what he was doing, (farming) try something else and get the bank off his back! I shook his hand on a tough decision made in time for him!

Friend, you are NOT, I am NOT a failure because what we tried didn't work. We pick up the pieces today from our mistakes and move on. Life is what you make it: decisions. Better ones daily will lead to a better life. A life of peace!

You know what is hard I believe for any farmer unlike other types of businesses is that we have conditions that are many times out of our control. The weather conditions can run havoc on your crops even if you have livestock as your primary source, you still need feed, and if weather is bad from where those farmers farm your pricing will be affected which will affect your profit margin for that season and many times for years. Now some could say you plan with those contingencies, I agree now, but when you're handed a farm as a legacy you don't always get that training, or you might not have that as a luxury, it's a serious business, this farming. It's not like perhaps the way it was when my grandfather was farming. With technological advances and the cost of farming getting so out of reach in order to remain competitive, let alone just on target, and within budget, well add that with the dynamics of culture and rearing, and just living... You get the picture; you see what the man mentioned above was facing, as do many of you, and many of you who may not be farmers.

For years I have suffered under negative thoughts that told me I was no good because I had failed as a result of not living up to the standards set by my grandfather and my father. My grandfather had started with nothing and owned 7 farms and stockyards when he died. My father started with everything and owned nothing when he died.

Before 5 years ago I would not have written that because my pride of who my family is or was would have prevented it. I write it now because who I am and who my family is now is who we are. I don't have to 'look good' any more.

Being good and true to self leads to becoming a person who is true and good to others.

My family is a good family. But we were raised to judge people by what they had their possessions more than about who they were. A choice I have made is this: People I now associate with are there for people like me, not for the money. When we lived in the apartment we had few visitors. The only people interested in talking to us sincerely were creditors and a very few friends and family. I am not judging. Unfortunately when the chips are down, self-inflicted or not, you discover who your real friends and close family are. At the time of writing I struggled financially. I am now a wealthy man financially Thanks to God!

By the time you read this book friend I am a very wealthy man in ALL areas of my life.

Because I now understand the concept of wealth and prosperity by the One Who Created the idea in the first place; our Heavenly Father, for His idea of wealth is not just monetary, that's only a portion of the pie, for who cares if you're rich but like what I said I was dealing with in my life, if within your family your kids are on drugs trying to escape their reality by numbing it out. Or if you're rich and me and my wife are in constant turmoil with one another, at odds all the time, trying to kill each other, even if it's slowly. How about if you're rich and you're given a diagnosis of death in three to six months, do you care about the money? No in fact you'll spend every dime of it trying to live. Or I'm rich but I never see home or bed until I fall on it dead tired, now many of you may have similar circumstances, let me tell you that's not wealthy by God's standards. Remember the *"The Enemy hath come to kill, steal and destroy",* by whatever means necessary. If he can tie you up where you're so busy that you don't even see sickness coming, or you're so stressed that you didn't see the addiction coming, by whatever means necessary. You must get this guy's (the Devil's) MO (Mode of operation). He tries nothing new. Everything he does is recycled from our parents, grandparents, and from before them. Why because it's always worked. (John 10:10)

We must begin to see what's really of value- it's our lives! It's those things that make us feel like life is worth living for. You know your spouse, your children, your family, and your dog. What you do (work) provides income, and the ability to get shelter from the cold, hot, and extremes of conditions, they're great, but they can change, the aforementioned should be consistent, you know that which we truly place value upon and with our family and loved ones. With that said, I have decided to live my life and focus on good not evil. Positive, not negative, others not self. I have a great Counselor. He guides me through the still deep waters of life. He helps me consider what I need to consider and say what I need to say as a healed man of God.

For example, I decided to begin the rest of my life at 50 years of age. Friend, it's never too late, NEVER, to focus on the good things with a bright, open and unchartered future ahead with Christ at the helm.

My recent boss appeared to be genuine and in my corner, it was a first time for me. Prior to and during this time there were always hidden agendas and interests. That's just the way in companies. They are good people. They just never really got to know me. I leave when I am not listened to. All the financial services industry tests and scores told me that I wasn't "employee" material. I am still an entrepreneur.

I can remember in the last corporate role I had, as a result of restructuring, half of my responsibilities in my role had disappeared. Many (yes, you friend) may have said GREAT!! 50% (half) job for 100% the pay!!

I guess I am different. I need 100% challenge for 100% of the pay.

I decided to leave 1 year later because I felt I was misunderstood, not listened to. When my previous employer reprimanded me and told me to spend more time, (in clear view of everyone within the office) I was devastated. They didn't listen. They didn't care about the person, they apparently only a cared about their own agenda. I decided to leave at that point. I have forgiven them as well. I have spoken to them since then as well. All is well now. I do not harbor unforgiveness. Unforgiveness is a blessing blocker of the greatest magnitude; I go where I am celebrated not tolerated, you should too.

A good decision at the time was to leave. I was an entrepreneur but the details bogged me down and so I struggled with the details and attempts to create my own structure & systems to help me maintain order.

I needed someone else to provide the structure and help look after the details. I regress.

Decide to win.
Decide to get around positive people.
Decide to get around people with your best interests in their heart.
(I have His name and her name is Sue)

Decide to read great books.
Decide to live life.
Decide to focus on a great goal.
Decide to see the good.
Decide to pray and meditate and realize it is not about me (or you).
Procrastination pushes life away.

Friend, don't procrastinate. At the time of writing I am two years from the time I had promised Mr. Les Hewitt, co-author of the book The Power of Focus with Mr. Jack Canfield and Mr. Mark Victor Hansen, (The Chicken Soup for the Soul authors) to complete and send him a copy of this book and my first book, The Wealthy Farmer in September 2004. I haven't done it yet. What's with that? Procrastination kills dreams, goals, anything in its way. (Read John 10:10 again)

Friend, I got that term from Pastor Joel Osteen's new book "Your Best Life Now"
It is a MUST read!! Available in book stores now.

 I am, for this chapter writing this book on vacation (paid for by the company) looking across the pool at a group of people dancing, including a resort worker dressed in a Santa Claus suit carrying a sign "on Vacation". I love it.

Procrastination steals life.

The guy in the Santa Claus suit is funny but he is holding me back from getting this book completed.

The bottom line, if something isn't important enough to us we don't complete it, we procrastinate about it by dragging our feet, it's not a priority.

What happens?
The people we want to encourage (you friend) don't get encouraged because the book, The Wealthy Farmer Diary took too long a time to get finished!

I began writing this book in July 2002; it is now August 2007.

I had set a goal. Publish and distribute on September 2006 (oops!), our 30th wedding anniversary. Praise God! She is one fine woman. My wife Susan, whom I love dearly, deserves a medal for sticking it out with me for that long- She really does. It's a miracle.

Chapter 14 - The Little Stuff

When it comes to recognition there is no better reward than a heart felt "Good Work". Your efforts are appreciated! "Well Done" and "Hallelujah!"

You can tell if these words of encouragement are true for the long term or the short term by the actions of the leader in between. If he/she is helping you to achieve great or greater results and forgetting about themselves, (selfless), or their personal agenda, then you can follow them. If, however, they are 'pushing' their own agenda daily, they are in it for themselves. Personally, I have worked for a handful of people over my career as a farm boy, accountant in training, accountant and now in sales. I am not judging or criticizing, only- observing.

I believe true leaders "go through" adversity and trials and perform equally as well digging through the pile of poop as they do in walking through a beautiful garden.

I was once hired long ago as a student in accounts due to a good work ethic. I would rather (remember I am a farm boy and like to work hard!) go prime tobacco vs. drawing unemployment for more money and sitting at home. People see and appreciate good work ethics, and that got me the next job.

In recent years I was hired to work for a company in sales for the first time. I would be selling a prepaid tax consulting service. I have a good team leader and a many excellent mentors and successful peers to learn from. My current leader is one who is good at building teams. He is tough when he has to be, but very kind, and always thoughtful. He is a blessing in my life. Whenever I reflect on the way my team leader treated me in the past, tears well up in my eyes. God wants us to prosper (Jeremiah 29:11) and

He also sends people to us to help us when we don't know or can't find the way alone.

I worked for a good company with good people some of who were good leaders.
They do the little things.
Tend to the little stuff.
It wasn't always that way with them but they have become a better company on their way to very good as a result of better leadership.

I received a bonus, a good financial reward in recent months but that pales in comparison to the shirt with the company logo and the pen with which I write these words (that I showed everyone before I gave it away!) My team leader wrote a note on the box that said, "Good work David…Keep the "money rolling" and signed his name. That meant the world to me. Someone was grateful for my efforts. Someone recognized me as a person. Someone took the time to encourage me. Money is important. It's not about the money.

I have a financial mentor as well, who knows when to pick up the phone to encourage me. These people are precious, very precious people in my life. I have recently engaged a personal coach as well. One who keeps me on track; he helps me overcome the frustrations, to continue focused and set aside all barriers that would hold me back from a life lived with passion. A life lived to the fullest keeps me excited about the future!

There was a time in very recent days, and as early as two years ago before engaging a debt counseling service when my own accountant (and friend) and my financial planner also my friend, and counselor are all telling me to file personal and corporate bankruptcy to clear away the mistakes brought on by very poor decisions of the past. I will never enter into anything like that by choice. I cast that care unto God. Psalm 89 tells me God's Will. I take God literally. They are paid now that this book has become a best seller across the country. They (my financial counselors and friends) can't deal with the stress of the debt, as they don't have the faith and conviction in God to resolve all of this like I do. It has nothing to do with pride, nothing! They want what is best for David and his family and I understand and appreciate their sincere concern. They simply don't share in the faith to believe that even when it's this bleak that it can turn around. It has already spiritually and now naturally. It's over and done by God's standards, not mans, Praise God!!

How did things get so bad?
I used my heart instead of good sound judgment or informed decision-making. I thought I had a right to be in business for myself…no matter what. Wrong or as Wayne in Wayne's World said it "NOT"! I have the right to make

informed decisions and be an entrepreneur but I don't have the right to be in business if I am not finding ways to become more productive in team and profit building. I chased after the dream and it almost ruined me financially and mentally (nothing was working).

Somewhere in there the little stuff, the details the things that give or enhance your effectiveness that stuff my grandfather knew, the stuff I some how missed or didn't fully understand it's significance in business, or I just didn't want to do. I understand now that the little things, the little stuff are self-esteem builders. This little stuff counts. It's the core foundation; you know the threading that makes the fabric.

One must become little before one becomes great. One must experience humility prior to greatness.

Chapter 15 - More Faith

"Faith comes by hearing, and hearing by the Word of God"
(Romans 10:17)

I have talked about a lot of things so far, but now it is time for faith.

"For without faith it is impossible to please God "
(Hebrews 11:6)

It is faith in God that keeps me alive. Without faith the blow of the cancer diagnosis would have been a knock out punch.

I spoke in earlier chapters about decisions that we all make, some good some not so good...

I decided to *"choose life"* as God's Word says in Deuteronomy 30:19, *"I have set before you life and death, blessing and cursing. Therefore, <u>choose</u> life."* *You do have a <u>choice</u>.*

I chose Life after the cancer diagnosis. Cancer will not and cannot kill me. My faith in God and the decision I have made to trust in Him and to fully appreciate that He is bigger than any disease, is to choose to live because what you think of and about yourself will and can ultimately kill you. But when you choose to let God work out the details and help you- help yourself, then you are choosing life as stated in Deuteronomy 30:19. Your choice affects your children's, children's, children, as seen by my life, for I'm proof positive that family decisions are a legacy, what's decided will determine if it's a good one or a bad one, what of you friend?

Friend, I know what you're thinking right now. You're thinking: "but I have lost a friend or family member to that dreaded disease." I lost my Father to prostate cancer. I know and empathize with you. Everyone has a decision to make on what we allow to transcend our peace. My decision is different than my fathers or your family member or friends. I have decided to trust my Heavenly Father's Words in **Isaiah 53:5-6**, **1 Peter 2:24-25** and **Matthew 8:17** Where it says that Jesus our Lord and Savior took on all our diseases, bore our iniquities, frailties, shortcomings, everything so that we might have faith in Him and really WIN!

When we put our faith in what the Word of God says about and for us then we win consistently. Christ conquered death and its entire sting; End of it- done! Jesus' last words on earth *"It is finished"*. I did, however, participate in traditional medicine and they have played a key role in my life and its length. (See Psalm 91)

I will tell you my story about my own healing and the building of my faith. It has been easier to believe for healing up until now than for financial prosperity. That's just me.

About a year after my diagnosis in 2002, I spoke words of faith about my situation in the presence of my radiation oncologist. I said, "I have authority from the highest power that I am healed and that cancer will not kill me." His reply: "We will monitor you for another year or so and keep you on hormone therapy until WE WHIP THIS (cancer) THING!"

A very key point here is this: I released my faith, AND THEN my doctor released his. I believe he would have never had spoken those words had I not first released my words of faith first in God's ability to heal me, RIGHT THEN!!! I pray at this point you are truly listening. Please re-read the previous few paragraphs again, find the **three scriptures** I referred to and meditate on them, asking God's Holy Spirit to reveal His awesomeness to and through you.

This is worth repeating. I decided to live. Many decide they will die and do. That is between them and God. I decided to build up my faith. I decided that I would study all of Kenneth E. Hagin's ministry writing's on faith, healing and prayer founded and rooted in and on the Word of God. I've been doing that over the past 5 years. It has truly blessed me. I AM HEALED! Praise God! I am no longer the same. I decided to turn toward God's Word and away from man's word.

Man is limited. I have done some of my own research as to why some born again, faith-filled, healing believing Christians have died prematurely. The primary reason… they couldn't get rid of a diagnosis that contained subtle, fearful, "authoritative", educated, professional, FINAL SOUNDING words of death. Those words became larger to them than God's words. That, for them, was the knock out punch that they couldn't recover from.

Faith fills life. Fear: "**F**alse **E**vidence **A**ppearing **R**eal" breeds doubt and unbelief and drains life right out of your very existence. You can decide to Live FULL OF FAITH or die EMPTY OF FAITH, and fearful, doubtful and in unbelief. The opposite of Faith is fear. But *"perfect love casts out fear"* (1 John 4:18).

Faith has me here. God has me here. Love has me. Faith Fills.

God is pleased with my faith. I must stay plugged into His word or I will surely perish. God's Word is Life.

Chapter 16 - Love

1Co 13:1: "What if I could speak all languages of humans and of angels? If I did not love others; I would be nothing more than a noisy gong or a clanging Cymbal".

1Co 13:2: " What if I could prophesy and understand all secrets and all knowledge? And what if I had faith that moved mountains? I would be nothing, unless I loved others."

1Co 13:3: "What if I gave away all that I owned and let myself be burned alive? I would gain nothing, unless I loved others."

1Co 13:4: " Love is kind and patient, never jealous, boastful, proud, or rude.

1Co 13:5: Love isn't selfish or quick tempered. It doesn't keep a record of wrongs that others do".

1Co 13:6: "Love rejoices in the truth, but not in evil."

1Co 13:7: " Love is always supportive, loyal, hopeful, and trusting".

1Co 13:8: " Love never fails! Everyone who prophecies will stop, and unknown languages will no longer be spoken. All that we know will be forgotten".

1Co 13:9: " We don't know everything, and our prophecies are not complete."

1Co 13:10: "But what is perfect will someday appear, and what isn't perfect will then disappear."

1Co 13:1: "When we were children, we thought and reasoned as children do. But when we grew up, we quit our childish ways."

1Co 13:12: "Now all we can see of God is like a cloudy picture in a mirror. Later we will see him face to face. We don't know everything, but then we will, just as God completely understands us."
1Co 13:13: "For now there are faith, hope, and love. But of these three, the greatest is love."

What I appreciate most about 1 Corinthians the Thirteenth chapter is that it is the cornerstone to life. When it shares the principles or characteristics of what love is you learn that it really is as God is, for God is Love. (1 John 4:8) He embodies all that He wishes us to experience, and by doing so we can have a deep intimate relationship with Him and truly experience Him. For His love is unconditional without pre-favors, no smoke and mirrors, nothing you have to do to receive love for. But this type of love (Agape' Unconditional Godly) is foreign to us, for when we are born we look for someone to love us. You can go to 1st, 2nd and 3rd John and interchange God for the word Love. A world without Love is a wasteland. If we don't have God/Love in our hearts we cannot love others.

When I attended Westover's co-dependency 7-day program with 6 other people adversely affected by drug and alcohol addiction through a family member, I discovered an important truth. I didn't love myself. In my mind's eye, because I hadn't become a successful and wealthy man by the age of 50 - that I was not lovable because (at the time for years leading up to that time), in my own mind, I was a loser. That was a lie from the Devil. I learned to not only like myself but as well I also learned to love myself. If your heart is empty it cannot give of itself to others.

My wife, along with my son is the reason I went to Westover for co-dependant counseling. My wife loved my son so much through his time of drug addiction that she used funds unaware to me at the time to pay off drug dealers who threatened to hurt or kill either; my son or her and or other family members if my sons unpaid drug debts weren't met.

This was a mother's love for her child; it, love, saw nothing else but to help a son the best way she knew how. The drug dealers should have been exposed instead of hidden from me and paid off. I struggled with this situation for a long time. Why was this a problem you may say, partly because this was a situation that I didn't have control over. I hated not being able to protect my son from the vices of this addiction, or to protect my wife. It's truly frustrating when you believe you're doing or have done your best, yet despite your best efforts, there are still things out of your control that leave you paralyzed.

Friend, have you ever tried to control a situation involving a family member that you couldn't control? It's tough isn't it? We want to love our family but we also want to control (as fathers) the family as the head of the family.

It just occurred to me that God is in control, not myself. I need to seek His Word about being the head of the family and live His Word. I love my wife. I love my sons and my daughter. I need to, as you probably do as well, to review 1 Corinthians 13 daily until we get it. We should insert our name in the place where we read the word "love".

Chapter 17 - Daily Attitudes

For years I have lived in a negative thoughts world. The enemy (that is Satan and he is real) has controlled too many of my thoughts, my habits, my day, my life. I get tired thinking about all I have voluntarily given up in my life for well over 40 years. Round and 'round and 'round I go around the mountain in the desert on the way to the promise land; put there with the help of the enemy, watching to see where we idle in our actions produced by our thoughts, (Satan the devil). He is a loser, but we (I) don't have to lose with him any longer. He wants many to lose with him. Again: *"Kill, steal and destroy."* (John 10:10)

We are to renew our minds with God's Word daily. I start each day praying for 15 minutes and spend time with God in His Word. These are my best days.
Distractions and poor attitudes that are virtually meaningless keep us from our best life.

I am a kind, loving, thoughtful person who loves people. No doubt I appear to be a thoughtless jerk to my wife, family, friends and business associates at times because I've been so preoccupied by my personal financial state. This was caused by my inability to save money coupled with falling into the trap of impulse spending which only brings with it the issues of shame, guilt and lost joy. While at Westover, this became abundantly clear to me.

Westover Counseling Center was a blessing; due to my sons addiction it taught me a great deal about myself.

We must decide EVERY DAY to live a life of gratitude for what we have and not dwell on the mistakes of the past.

I must purpose in my heart daily to renew my mind with God's word. It is absolutely imperative!

1John 4:4: *"Greater is He that is in thee than He that is in the world!"*

Hallelujah!

Chapter 18 - Humility & Obedience

On October 12, 2005, I am back to write a few more chapters before publishing this book. This is something that has taken me a long, long time to learn. Not being able to be humble has cost me the family home, my business and almost cost me my family. I was born a Brown and where I 'came' from (Shedden, Ontario Canada) that name 'meant something'. I am thankful for my heritage, a hardworking, giving successful Grandfather and a strong disciplinarian father, but I am not 'proud' of the name anymore. (That's another story). It is just that…a name. For almost 30 years I tried to do 'it' - that is, become successful by my own strength and develop wealth. For 30 years "financial wealth" has eluded me and the only thing I was good at was accumulating and developing debt and growing financial problems for everyone close to me.

When I reflect on the latter aspect of my financial life and where I believe it's rooted Romans 8:1 comes to mind. *"There is now no condemnation for those who are in Christ."* That's me and can be you if you receive that scripture as yours too.

Let's talk about humility. I mean let's *really* talk about humility. Let's get right down to it. No holds barred. All bet's are off. No turning back. Here it goes….

A great deal of it…humility was developed the day I sat in a doctor's office and he told me what he thought cancer would do to me. "You will probably wind up the way your father went". That is to say, full of disease and pain. My father made a decision however that although his body may have been riddled with cancer, this prognosis didn't mean he'd have to give his eternal life and be dammed forever. One week before he died my father accepted Jesus as his Lord and Savior and his Redeemer. So God gained another: Stewart Brown-1, Satan-0.

My dad made a motion with his hand and arm to slap the lid shut on the coffin, and to throw the dirt into the grave figuratively. Realistically he was ready to go he had had enough. This is the picture that came to mind when the doctor spoke words of fear, doubt and pain. I cried for 2 weeks. I was humbled. Oh yes, the day I was diagnosed I was hit by a car in Tim Horton's parking lot talk about being humbled, not that this is or that any of the bad things that happen to us are from or are of God, instead you're humbled because you realize that yes bad things happen to good people.

Ecclesiastes 9:11 says: "I returned to see
under the sun that the swift do not have the
race, nor the mighty ones the battle, nor do the
wise also have the food, nor do the
understanding ones also have the riches, nor
do even those having knowledge have the
favor; because time and unforeseen
occurrence befall them all." We are all subject
to bad things happening to us. But the humbling
perspective should be just how fragile and
precious time is regarding our lives, for we don't
know the day nor the hour of when that final
curtain call happens. **'Lights, Camera,**
Action!' You're on- this is your life episode
you fill in the number, oh didn't anyone
tell you, there are no dress rehearsals, this is
a live feed, God is watching. The only One
that really matters that you want to see your
performance is HIM!

We become humbled realizing that we are as
dust in the wind, we our lives are fragile and to
be treasured by and for what matters most.
Again I say life, and who gives us life-God!

After the initial diagnosis, came the treatment
and cure. I received radiation for 6 weeks and
then female hormones to shut down the
testosterone for 3 years. Need I say more?
Humbled.
Humbled again.

Next comes my current employer. My current employer was a company I had sold against and criticized because of a weak service and reporting model that lead to poor decisions by farmers. I had approached them for a job as a field account or MSR (Member Service Representative) as they are called. I completed a survey for them.

I flunked it? I was not qualified to be one of their field accountants. What was that?

I thought I had written a 'best selling' book about financial management. I had been a corporate field controller and a corporate credit manager and have the letters CMA after my name, which stands for Certified Management Accountant. For crying out loud I was an individual with a professional accounting designation and I DID NOT QUALIFY to be a field accountant for this company I previously disliked. I was SURE that I would become a tremendous producer for them. I did it before. Not to happen.

You guessed it. Humbled. Humbled. Humbled.

By this time, after all of this, I began to get the picture. Get rid of self and walk in humility.

When my son began using cocaine it literally turned our home and my marriage upside down for a period of almost 3 years. He never said why.

Everywhere I turned I was getting slapped, pushed, shoved, yelled at, wrestled, manipulated, and let DOWN.

So I finally began to realize that what I was doing wasn't working. It wasn't. Nothing was…working. But some ONE was. God was. God was changing me and developing a soft heart within me I had begun to yield to someone that I felt had to have some answers or at least a way for me to deal, and cope, because our life was out of control.

So after a couple of months of my current employer not calling, I HUMBLED MYSELF and CALLED THEM.

I was asked to come in for an interview. I thought…they have finally come to their senses and they NEEDED ME TO HELP THEIR ACCOUNTANT TEAM!
WRONG!!!!! SO WRONG!!!! When I got there I was told I flunked the field accountant test but there was an opening in sales if I would like to "give that a whirl!"

Well, I had just finished the Colors Course (planning for change) and discovered that I was no longer an accountant by those tests. This test confirmed it. I started in sales and marketing and I loved it. God is blessing me BIGTIME. He got me (for a season) where He wanted me, and had given me my strongest abilities in. See

Matthew 25:13-30: *"And to each one He gave talents according to their abilities."* I am developing my communication AND PATIENCE AND LISTENING SKILLS. I SEE A FAIR BIT OF REJECTION. It comes with the territory. The bottom line, because I got (or fell off) my "high horse" and became humble, I am blessed. It works. Some are slower (me) than others to catch on but watch out now, it's all about *"Him who supplies all my needs according to His riches and Glory." Glory Be to God! Glory Be to God!!*

Chapter 19 - Love, and Encouragement

Topic – Money

This has to be the all time emotional trigger for most people. Unfortunately, money management is not taught by most parents or by the educational system.

I am the type, the rogue, the maverick, the; "odd-ball" the "different one" who attends all of the meetings and gets all pumped and fired up. I remain changed for a time, only to become confused and frustrated when I can't find or duplicate that "state" "euphoria". Consequently,

I spiral further down a dark pit of debt, frustration, pain, anguish, despair, hopelessness and fear. Who or what are we connecting to when this happens?

Because of the struggle I have experienced in the areas of debt, drugs and disease it has brought me to a place of humility. Understanding my frailties I am now able to truly be of service. God states in His Word in the book of 1 Corinthians 1:26-29: ***"God chose the weak things of the world, that He might put the strong things to shame; and why; in order that no flesh might boast in the sight of God".*** "When the student is ready the Teacher will appear", to be a student one must first yield and submit to the one teaching, so you can learn something, I'm learning a whole lot now.

Let me explain. In the summer of 2005, I read a book that has changed my life. After I read it I immediately enrolled in a 3-day seminar 2 hours from where I live, for early that November.

My wife Susan went with me. (One of a handful of times she has come with me in her life). I believe she knew in her heart we needed to be together on this one. She was right, she was so right.

We left early on Friday morning and arrived early to the seminar/course and therapy, this life-changing event. Let me stop right here and clarify it was NOT a 'religious' event, a cult or MLM meeting. It was a journey into the bowels of our very beings that we were both very ready for. Our souls needed a positive spin. The students were ready and the teachers appeared.

What started out as a 'seminar' concluded as a very high impact gut-wrenching, emotional release of 30 years of junk for both my wife and I and the 'issues' and emotions we both had developed (all negative) around money. What we were "putting out" into to the "Universe" was coming back to us…namely, debt and financial lack! Consistently. It was working "against" and not for us. The movie "The Secret" comes back to mind.

We arrived early and I was immediately drawn to one the event staff members, Bob. He shared that by the end of the second day I would no longer be the same person, nor would be for the rest of my life.

He was off by half a day. It was the Sunday morning on that third day that I had my real breakthrough. The Facilitators of the "seminar" asked us to write down all of the life- time negative feelings and issues, emotions we had developed and concluded about the topic of money. We then had to face our partner and tell them what we had written and we were instructed to "feel" the whole, entire, huge emotions that we had suppressed around the subject of money.

I can only share what I experienced, not what my wife did, or what I heard about anyone else there. I had interacted positively with at least one third of 1,400 people in attendance, in a very positive and emotional way. I was probably crying.

I have been to plenty of "RAH- RAH" shows before but not **REAL** like this was!

My wife had "used" tens of thousands of dollars to help our son deal with his cocaine addiction and the problems it brought with it. Now before anyone judges her just hear me out. My wife has been condemned by just about everyone she knows including me.
He or she who has never sinned may cast the first stone. But again I truly believe even those who condemned my wife for her mothers love, her unconditional "I'm saving my son's life love, I'll pay whatever, and no amount of condemnation or judgment will give me my son back if I don't pay these ******* you knows, you know!"

She did, as I'm sure almost all mothers and fathers would have in those circumstances. It's easy to say what you'd do when you're not in, you know 20/20 hind site, but up close and personal, you don't envision your child no matter how old in a coffin, even if it's one they're apparently digging for themselves. Our son has been judged guilty and condemned by just about everyone he knows, including me. Now we will set Dustin aside at this point. He WAS an addict. An activity performed separate from who the person is, verses what the person does, or yields to through weakness, like many of you, maybe yours isn't your perception of life, thus addictions to escapism, perhaps it's control, or perfection, next to someone who doesn't want to be controlled or doesn't want your perfection, you're a nut case to them too.

Do you recognize the name from the first book? Dustin was the main character...The Wealthy Farmer. He still is...The Wealthy Farmer. He had a problem, so did Susan.
I love them both no matter what. Love -1.
Judging & Condemnation – 0. Love wins!
Romans 8:1 (again)

Let's focus on Susan for a moment.

What a terribly horrible, emotionally empty, negatively charged, despairing, lost, dark, guilt-ridden, shame-filled, esteem-less place was she in at the moment of those decisions to support the addict in her life, her son, and turn her back on others after 50 years of living.

Stop right here.

If any of you are condemning Susan at this point that will come right back to bite you in the back side! Do you really understand the point I am making? She was at the end of her emotional rope.

I SAW and HEARD that emotion on Sunday morning. I heard and saw the utter despair in her voice and watched her shake before I broke down into an emotional cry I have NEVER had before in my life. I was sobbing to the point I was losing my breath! I have had loved ones die in our family and NEVER have I cried and let emotion out like this!

To see someone you love reflect her darkest moments is real humility. I am sensing that emotion again right now as I write this down even while I sit and glance at the peaceful waters of Lake Erie at the beach in Port Stanley, Ontario.

Now...are you ready for more. If not, set the book down, take a deep breath and come back to it. Meditate on the times you have condemned someone or judged someone NEVER KNOWING WHAT WAS GOING ON IN THEIR HEADS OR LIFE at the time! If this is so, ask for forgiveness and if the person has gone on, please REWRITE THE STORY! It's *your* story!

What else was going on in my head?

After a time I composed myself and shared what was going on with me. Amazingly, as I began to write this segment the sun came out and warmed me.

I had written down that I was upset with my father that he had not left me an inheritance like his father left him. We were both first-born sons. Had I inherited it, I would have spent it. Irony right? Nevertheless, I was carrying around all of the garbage of debt, impulse spending, cancer issues, and the inability to provide for family in later years JUST LIKE MY FATHER!

As I shared, I realized something deep... very, very deep. I loved and still love my father. He loved and still loves me!

(*This is an aside, but as I am writing I saw a young man sitting alone on the beach thinking and looking out at the water and after a while his wife or girlfriend showed up and they reconciled right in front of me. Love and forgiveness heals. Love brought peace there.)*

I just had to include that piece because that is why this book got written and published. Love and forgiveness!

As I began to share about my father, a terrible negative emotion containing so much fear,

worry, anxiety, doubt, anguish and everything
you can use to describe the time when you were
at your uttermost darkest place came upon me.
A bad feeling- YES! Was this feeling a good
thing? YES!

What I experienced, and came to realize, was
this. My earthly father never experienced
financial freedom in his life. Ever. The money
always came from one of two places: either
inheritance or debt. I had experienced one of
these and felt ripped off. That is because of my
choices it was the latter.

The pain of financial lack, debt, losing
everything and I do mean "Everything" was
horrendous. Months before my Dad died, WAS
WORSE for my earthly father than the PAIN
OF THE CANCER that KILLED MY FATHER
in April of 1998. Did you get that?

My father was in more anguish over his inability
to provide, not from a lack of education, not
from a lack of a good start, not from the lack of
being able to express himself well in front of a
large group of people. I T WAS THE NEVER
ENDING PAIN OF BEING IN DEBT THAT
HE NEVER CONQUERED IN HIS
LIFETIME.

People can have an ending with disease and
even death. But most people live in a debt

plagued destructive life of debt all their lives; these, as I used to be, can/never SEE THEMSELVES FINANCIALLY FREE.

The freedom that my father desired will be lived out in my lifetime. Not even the siblings in our family who are set up well financially will ever realize the victory like the writer will because THEY HAVEN'T BEEN THERE! This is not a slam but a fact!
The curse has been lifted and the blessings are here now!

I thank God for that life changing experience.

The fact that this book is published and a best seller is testimony of the success I now enjoy. Financial freedom. Walking in such Love and Faith that fear, debt and disease are behind me.

Glory to God!

Chapter 20 - More about the money…

Money is not only a material or worldly issue it is also a spiritual one. In the bible there are 2,350 scripture references to money. You think this book knows a few things about the subject?

I am 52 years of age and I am finally taking the steps of faith to walk from debt to wealth. Being in Debt and being a servant to the lender has been my way of life up to this point. God's word says in the book of 1st Timothy 6:10 *...The LOVE of money is the root of all evil, and one bible version (NWT) puts it this way: "For the love of money is a root of all sorts of injurious things, and by reaching out for this love some have been led astray from the faith and have stabbed themselves all over with many pains. "* Well I can testify to that scenario, and I'm sure many of you will sing a few Amen's to that also. It's horrible what our desire to be successful will lead us into or I should say our perception of it.

The bible also says; *"that man cannot have two masters for he will serve one and hate the other".* For most of my adult life I was truly serving the one who has you going through life moaning, groaning and complaining about everything you have, even though you signed up for it. You know that part of the contract that ties not only your life up but your families too. I have lived above my means and borrowed to drive newer vehicles and keep myself in everything such as coffee, eating out, entertainment, books, tapes and vacations. All of these things not bad in themselves but were beyond my means. I budgeted infrequently. I had read every book there was on personal finances and investing including "The Wealthy

Barber". I have been temporarily influenced in the past to save some money but not enough where it would get me out of debt. Yet even with all the various books, tapes, seminars and even more, heck I'm a CMA, but it still didn't change how I thought I was supposed to look, even though inside I knew I wasn't the type of success I really desired, if it's really not yours you don't own it and as I mentioned earlier you're a slave to it.

I now understand that when the Lord calls and leads you follow. I'm a Canadian living in St. Thomas, Ontario. In my quest to please God and completely allow Him to be at the helm of my life verses me continuing to navigate through the rocky and tumultuous waters, (seeing I've made such a mess of it), am now following Him where ever He may send me. And a test of that faith did come. He led me to a church that for all intense and purposes I under my natural influences would not have gone, but God does know where to send us for growth. Remember that passage I quoted earlier from James 4: 1-3, *"you get not because you ask for a wrong purpose."* I had always been asking for a wrong purpose, for sensual pleasures the 'me, me, me' requests. Well I'm done with all that, I'm in His purpose, I ask for whatever You (God) see me doing, sense He sees it anyway, just let me in on it, you know. Well He did, and sent me across the border to the United States of America in Southfield, Michigan. I'm now a member at a place that is educating me on life and finances exponentially.

I know I am in His will by attending this church. This is where I build my faith. This is where I grow spiritually and will become a minister who travels the world as an evangelist. This is where I recently completed an 8 week "Awesome" financial program called "Dominating Money" put on by the Kingdom Business Association hosted by an equally awesome Christian organization- Word Of Faith International Christian Center, www.woficc.com check them out on the web, they are doing a mighty work and move in The Lord worldwide. I travel to this center/church one way two hours on each travel for church on Sundays for worship and praise and Wednesdays for mid-week in-depth Bible services Shepherded by Bishop Keith A. Butler and a host of anointed Ministerial and Pastoral staff. I also travel again for the business school at the educational center of the church taught by the anointed Dr. Victor and Minister Catherine Eagan. The Kingdom Business Institutes program has 12 courses, 8 weeks in length, which can be completed over a 3-year period. The "Dominating Money" course has saved my life financially. The Eagan's come with God's love first, which is why our class and many others can receive knowledge from them so readily. This personal finance course was the most powerful one I have ever completed! Remember.... I am a certified accountant in Canada! The Eagan's are anointed to teach God's people about finances.

It had been easier for me to believe for healing from cancer than to believe, truly believe that I would ever become debt free until now! I have been in financial bondage for 30 years. Can any of you reading this book relate? The bondage of debt has been removed now. Mathew 11:28, Hosea 6:5; *"My people perish from a lack of knowledge"*.
The course and workbook "Dominating Money" Tapping into God's supernatural economy is the BEST I have ever studied. There is no grey in the materials. None!

It is black and white. I have a knowing beyond understanding from their teaching and experience, which is powerful. The reason "it is working" for me is that I observed and have absorbed their genuine love for me before I observed and absorbed their teachings for me. Don't get me wrong I'm not knocking any other financial programs out there, but if you really want to be set free from debt and the attitudes that permeate placing us in continual bondage then you will also want to make the trek across the water, *as the **Apostle Peter said: "Lord if it be you, bid me to walk on the water"*** (Matthew 14:28) and get in this program, look on-line on the website listed and key in KBI, (Kingdom Business Institute).

This program works because it's God's perspective, He's got the manual on life, if we just read it He will unlock doors and it is my wish and prayer for you today that if you take nothing else away from this book you get that God wants you "Wealthy" in all areas of your life from His perspective, and it's an awesome view. Think about it. Are you really at peace with all that you have, and if you lost it all today would you still be at peace? If what you're living for is not worth dying for then perhaps you're living for the wrong thing. I know I was, today if I left this earth I know I'm giving God all I have, the *"Whole soul, heart and mind"* part of the first command, what of you?

I am well on my way to becoming a Kingdom Millionaire! These are not just words in a book. This is a reality- first the spirit realm before the worldly realm. I believe, think and act like a Kingdom Millionaire. www.kingdommillionaire.com. I am going to move my author's pen from this to the next book. That book will detail my renewed mind that is grounded in God's word. I have the mind of Christ. Step by step.

Each important word, action, goal, belief, revelation and manifestation as it is and will occur in the process of me finally taking hold of the wealth I have always had spiritually but was deceived through debt, borrowing, overspending and giving in to discontentment involving material things. I have become a new man in every sense- materially and spiritually. I enjoy the peace that passes all understanding. I am at peace with my life. My finances, my health and focus on the final revelation that John 10:10 confirms that my life is to be abundant; *"For the enemy hath come to steal, kill and destroy, But (But God), I have come that you may have life more abundantly".* **I receive and believe that life now to the glory of God!** My mission is to further the Kingdom of God on earth. An experience that that I received as a blessing half way through the Dominating Money course was as follows:

We were all sitting intensely studying a video with Minister Catherine Eagan. So intense that we didn't stop for a break and the course leaders shut the video off at 9:15pm. Class ends at 9pm. It was near the 9pm mark that a young lady I had never met before, Kim Newsome awkwardly placed a wristband on my desk (she was sitting to my right and we had never met.) She placed the elastic bracelet in front of me in a very awkward manner. Quick and obedient, I spoke to her after class and she shared that God had told her to give her extra bracelet to the man beside her and that Minister Catherine Eagan and she had observed through praise and worship time how much I love the Lord. What she confessed had me realize that my heavenly Father is watching me and through this obedient servant (Kim) declared that he is watching over me. It dawned on me how much I really do love the Lord! I left the room into a stall in the men's room and broke down and sobbed for a long time. I lost my breath I was crying so hard. The debt burden had been taken off of me and the Wealthy place anointing came upon me right there! Praise God! I know it and confess it! For the first time in my life I have my financial house in order. The big course project for Dominating Money had me put ALL of my financial details into one binder.

My finances are now IN ORDER! Freedom, REAL FREEDOM from debt is now mine!

Chapter 21 - My Father-in-Law His Final Chapter here on earth

It was June of 2006. My father-in-law, Bill, was going in and out of the hospital. He was having seizures. He had a stroke about 5 years ago and it appeared to be strokes again.

Let's go back in time.

Let's go back 31 yeas ago when Bill first came into my life. I began dating his oldest daughter Susan. I had always noticed Susan, from a distance, in high school. She was the one you always wanted to go out with, but she was going steady with a tall, dark and "handsome" basketball player, so- no chance. No chance for a farm boy who wasn't athletic and had no apparent 'gifts'; certainly nothing that a young lady like Susan would be interested in.

I was a dork, not dorkey... a dork! I was a cigarette smoking, "to be cool" beer drinking (to be loud and heard) dork. No "cool" there. Yet.

I met Susan in a bar. She picked me up. I wasn't doing too good a job at focusing that particular evening. Friends, as you read these pages, you are picking up that God uses those of us who have learned humility after we were "cool" to create willing, obedient servants. God has an excellent, no, amazing sense of humor. He uses me! That in itself is a miracle. It really is.

Susan and I dated. A few months into the relationship, she gave me an emerald ring that I still wear today, my birthstone.

We fell in love. We were married on September 18, 1976, the year I graduated from University of Guelph with a Diploma in Agriculture. My peers fondly call me "A Dipper".

I have talked about the car accident in 1977, just one year after we were married. When I think of it, Bill probably didn't think much of me. Yet, somebody was praying for us.
I have a sense it was Bill's mother, Ann Hepburn. Ann was all peace, love and could

frequently be heard saying, "Good things come to those who wait". Susan and I often wondered how long we would have to ....wait. Ann's only daughter Donna is the "spitting image" of Ann, both beautiful people. My heart goes out to both Daphne my precious mother in law and Donna who lost both a husband and a brother (Bill) as well within 6 months. (Please pray for them reader.)

You know what? Good things are coming now. God is using me as His servant as He works through me to deliver others from their bondage of alcohol, drugs, lust, money, disease, worry and hopelessness each and every day.

Bill, my father-in-law, was a man of inner strength, knowledge, wisdom and a strong desire to succeed. He became a Certified General Accountant (CGA) after 8 years of intense correspondence courses. Bill managed 20 professional course credits in addition to the demands of 4 teenage daughters and a teenage son (Fergy) in their home. He had a knack of getting straight to the point, his ability to 'call a spade a spade', and his honest dealings with people; all of which influenced me profoundly. With Bill, you were never confused about where you stood. Ever.

Once, during a car purchase, (the one in the accident, Monte Carlo turned into Corvette in size) Bill turned to me and asked, "Why would you buy more debt?" I didn't listen and I have been, up until now, in debt ever since.

Reflecting back on Bill's life, I notice he always took the time for people. He may have worked a great deal as a husband and father while the children were young, but he took the time to attend the ballgames, hockey games, and go golfing with his eldest grandsons. He took the time. He made the time. He listened. There is no doubt in my mind that, as I jumped from idea to idea, opportunity to opportunity, Bill listened. He didn't always agree. His words sometimes sounded judgmental, but his responses, spoken in love, were always black and white.

A few years back, Bill was very worried about being diagnosed with cancer as a result of having his prostate removed 20 years ago. (There seems to be a lot of that around me)

God says in His Word in Psalm 91 that: *"1,000 may fall at your side, and 10,000 at your right hand, (remember) but it will not come near you."* I claim that scripture as my own.

David Brown will never die of cancer of any kind. I am anointed. I am whole. I am healed. I am walking under the Blood of Jesus. In Faith I trust Him. Mark 11:23-24, with the faith of a mustard seed you can move your mountains, with your faith in God's ability to give it to you

you'll have it, if it is as James 4:1-3 says: *"Asked for the right purpose."*

Bill was concerned 5 years ago about cancer. His worry brought on a stroke, which impaired his mobility. It took away things he loved, like big league base ball games and golf. Remember John 10:10: *"the enemy comes to kill, steal & destroy."* Am I using John 10:10, a lot, probably because Satan is doing it a lot, I want you to really understand that he's targeting you all the time, and all leaves nothing out.

It was June of 2006, Bill received the news that CT scans and x-rays revealed 3 lesions in his brain, and one growth in his lung with primary and secondary malignancy. Malignant, such an unwelcome word and one we never want to hear associated with cancer- a word second only to death which, paralyzes the recipients with fear. But I know a name above death and cancer. Jesus! Jesus! Jesus! The name of Jesus has power and authority over death and surely cancer. (Isaiah 53:5-6)

Believe what you want. I believe God and His Word. God gave us choice.

Bill was the man I talked to about everything. Business. Life. Work. Sports. Spirituality. Religion. Health. Family. Money.

He represented the generation before me. He was my mentor. I loved Bill. I love Bill and have an opportunity to continue loving him every time I love his daughter, my wife.

I remember the last time Bill was admitted to the hospital.

I remember watching my precious mother-in-law wilt under the weight of emotions, frustration, helplessness, discouragement, futility, and hopelessness. I witnessed her crumble as she came to realize Bill was beyond her help. Her lifetime role as wife, nurse, friend, lover, helper, coach, listener confidant and partner was slipping away right in front of her eyes.

There was no hope there because Jesus wasn't in that partnership. But Jesus was with me urging me to share Him with both Bill and Daphne.

On June 29, 2006 I was out and about in St. Thomas, Ontario.

I received a sense, in my spirit, to go visit Bill in the hospital. I didn't' want to. I was sad and, like everyone else 'in the flesh', feeling weakened. In spite of my reluctance, my spirit man (The Holy Spirit) took over and provided the strength I needed.

I almost turned left on 1st Ave at Elm Street, but instead, turned right and found myself driving to the Emergency parking lot at the hospital.

I sat quietly in the parking lot for half an hour and listened to the New Testament on my CD player. As I listened to Romans 3 through to 10, I was reminded of chapter and verse to Scripture, which leads us to accepting Jesus, becoming a Child of God resulting in our absolute Salvation. (Romans 10: 8,9,10)

It was after 9 pm before I entered the hospital, only to find the doors to the upper floors locked. Bill was on the 5th floor. Once again, I sat and prayed, this time for another half hour, asking the Lord to release a way to the 5th floor.

Friends, I was fighting both the flesh (which was tired and weak), spiritual darkness and principalities that wanted Bill to go to Hell and join them in torture.

These are the last days. I am not going to mince words. I am, as learned through Bill, "calling a spade a spade". The very same man, whom was directly responsible for coining that phrase for me, needed me to rise to the occasion.

Shortly after my prayer, a nurse walked past me and I motioned for her to let me through the locked doors; I continued praying in the Spirit as I took the elevator to the fifth floor.

I walked into Bill's room to find his roommate reading the newspaper, while Bill lay asleep in the darkness on the other side of the room. I couldn't help but notice the heaviness, both spiritually and physically, that engulfed the room.

Friends, you can't get to Heaven through good works or by being a member in good standing of a "Lodge" or Kiwanis Club. I am not taking aim at any organization or body. The fact is that until you accept Jesus into your heart as your Lord and Savior to be spiritually born again, your destination is Hell. (Joel 2, Romans 10)

Finishing the newspaper, Bill's roommate left the room and I walked in silence through the darkness over to Bill's bed.

Sensing my approach, Bill's eyes opened and he wakened to a light, which was radiating from within me, now permeating the darkened room. (Those of you who watch "Touched by an Angel" will have an understanding)

Seeing Bill awake, I was moved by love and led through tears, to tell him that I loved him. "I always have and I always will", I spoke. Bill looked me in the eyes. Numerous seizures had affected his voice and it was a strain for him to speak. I asked him if he wanted me to pray for him. He gasped his answer "yes" further nodding his head to ensure I understood. He asked if I was still going away on a business trip to Winnipeg, to which I replied, "later". Then I led him with these words…

"Heavenly Father, I pray for us. Bill... we are all sinners. We confess our sins now.
*We confess that Jesus came to die on the cross to save us from our sins. He is raised from the dead and is seated at; **"Your right hand."** We accept Jesus as our Lord and Savior."*

"Bill, do you accept Jesus as your Lord and Savior?"

I opened my eyes from prayer and turned to hear him gasp not once, not twice, but three times "Yes!" To the Father, Son & Holy Ghost!

Praise God!! Glory to God!! Hallelujah!! Thank You Jesus!!!

I prayed for peace for Bill, that his transition from this physical plane to the spiritual would be easy for him, and that he would have no more pain; a prophecy which came to pass.

I told Bill, again, that I loved him, that everything was okay now and that he was right with Jesus and his Heavenly Father. I reminded him that the Holy Spirit was with him and would continue to be during the death of his physical body.

God's plan for Bill's salvation was worked out that night. I went into the hallway, pumped my right arm and "Shouted YES!"

(Satan, you just lost another one! And many more to come on my watch!)

I left the hospital weeping with Joy!!

I called my friend, Shelly, and confessed, through tears what had happened. While doing that, the Holy Spirit fell on me with such an intense "heat" it was "incredible!" NEVER have I experienced that before. The fire burned intensely within my soul and body for a long time this time. I was so hot with the heat of the love of God that I wanted to remove all clothing at the time. I was uncomfortable in my own clothing. Amazing experience. He, The Holy Spirit, literally fell on me! I went home and told my wife that her father was on his way to Heaven. Only those who have experienced His love in this way know what I mean. It compares to nothing in the flesh.

Bill is with God now because of Gods Love, Grace and Mercy. Everything that Bill had done, up until that point, had not gained him eternity with God in Heaven.

"Ye must be born again" Glory to God!

Chapter 22 - Why the Wealthy Farmer Diary?

(To have you choose **life** not death)

It is time the truth comes out about our family and where we are. It doesn't have to look good from the road or highway.

This book was written to encourage people who have been oppressed by disease, drugs, and debt. It is a book about **HOPE**.

It is about encouragement, it is about loving those around you, it is about finding peace, love and hope. At the back of this book is a prayer called the Sinner's Prayer, which is a confession unto *"salvation"!*

Simple, you DECIDE to say that prayer from your heart and you accept Jesus Christ as your personal Lord and Savior and you immediately become a Born Again Christian. You have just received the Redemptive Gift of Christ Shed Blood as Sacrifice for your sins. What an awesome gift and opportunity for you to experience truly what it means to be forgiven and saved because He loves us first. God is reaching out to and for you take His hand and receive Everlasting Life!

The only way to the Father in Heaven is through Jesus Christ.

"I am the Way the Truth and Life and no one comes to the Father but by me" (John 14:6)

Thank you for taking the time to read and meditate on this book. (Read it twice or more, one needs repetition to truly meditate). I pray that the messages within encourage you and your families and friends and bring you hope for the future and abundant life. See John 10:10. Jesus wants you to join Him in abundance not lack!
1 John 4:4 *"Greater is He who is in me than he who is in the world."*

My confidence, my hope, my trust is in Him who is also my source and my savior. Look for future "Diary's" of how The Wealthy Farmer's future experiences and growth can continue to help you become the precious child of God that you are.

The next book *"From Minus To Millions In Months…. God's Way" will have a few chapters* on challenges but the bulk of that book will be a success testimony! Look for it very soon!

Sincerely,
David Brown
Humble, Obedient, Servant, Encourager

Glory Be To God!
Glory Be To God!
Glory Be To God Almighty!!!

A Sinners Prayer
To Receive Jesus as Savior
Dear Heavenly Father
I come to you in the Name of Jesus.

Your Word says: *"Him that cometh to me I will in no wise cast out"* (John 6:37), so I know "You" won't cast me out, but You take me in and I thank you for it.

You said in your Word: *"Whosoever shall call upon the name of the Lord shall be saved"* (Romans 10:13) I am calling on Your Name, so I know you have saved me now.
You also said: *"If thou shalt confess with thy mouth the Lord Jesus, and shalt believe in thine heart that God hath raised him from the dead, thou shalt be saved. For with the heart man believeth unto righteousness; and with the mouth confession is made unto salvation"* (Romans10: 9-10)

I believe in my heart that Jesus Christ is the Son of God. I believe that He was raised from the dead for my justification, and I confess Him now as my Lord.

Because Your word says: *"With the heart man believeth unto righteousness"* and I do believe in my heart, I have now become the righteousness of God in Christ (2 Corinthians 5: 21) ...And I am saved!

Thank You, Lord!

Signed...

_____

Date

_____

If you just prayed this prayer and accepted Jesus as your personal Lord and Savior let me be the first to say welcome inside the house of God. You have made the right choice, eternal life. To assist you with your decision our Heavenly Father has placed at your disposal caring Christian Volunteers who are available 24/hours a day, seven days a week waiting to couple their faith with yours. So no matter when you make that step towards the beginning of the rest of your life a loving and caring person is only a phone call away. Call 1-800-541-7729 at Word Of Faith International Christian Center. After speaking with you they will send some free information that will strengthen your personal relationship and spiritual walk and growth as a born again Christian with Christ Jesus our Lord and Savior- Praise God!

Epilogue

Is David Brown a finished product? Not even close. "My name is Jesse Brown, David's oldest son and the father to his only grandchild. I suggested he should be more proud of his success and his roots. So being the type of person Dad is he delegated this topic to me. There is one strength I will give to my father's credit, and that is that although he may have a great amount of enthusiasm for whatever drives him he does know what he can't do and therefore gets the proper people in place.

What can I say about my father that hasn't already been said? This book lays out all the trials and tribulations that he has gone through but doesn't touch some of the ideas and topics in his life that he should be most proud of.

Dad and Mom have been through more crap than I could ever imagine and that I hope I'll never go through with my wife. Did they make some wrong decisions? Yes. Did I agree on some of their decisions? No. But I am still their son and when it comes to the book you don't hear about me because Mom and Dad did a great job of getting me to a point where I could spread my wings and fly to become a good person and parent today. One of my dad and mom's greatest successes they have produced are their children. The love for their children and the amount of love they possess is second to none.

Dad does not give himself enough credit for his strong mind and when he chooses an idea or a venture, nothing and I mean nothing stops him. This has gotten him into trouble. No matter how much I have discussed his ideas with him he has already made up his mind. This again has cost him financially and emotionally. He may not be aware of this either but I figured with his ideas and my focus we could have been a great combination. Before I knew it the chance for us to work together was lost. I am like my Dad in many ways but when it comes to making a decision, Dad gets lost and can't see the forest from the trees. That was then. Now I see a focus and a passion more than ever before. He waits. He takes in all he can and keeps his emotions in check better than he ever has in the past.

Dad also does not talk about his current job. In the past, he bounced from corporate to self-employment, multi-level marketing schemes and back to the corporate world where he is the top selling sales person in his company. All his past failures make him a better person today. Dad knows what his faults are and is working around them to make him more successful and a better person, not just professionally but personally as well.

All in all, my Dad and entire family have been through a lot of trauma. I honestly believe that sometimes we don't realize all that has happened.

Am I proud of some of the things that have happened? No.
Am I still here learning from everything that has happened? Yes.
Can I continue to learn from the mistakes and life of my father? Absolutely.

If there is one thing that you can take from this book, it is that you are reading about a man that has died at least twice, should have died many times. Has lost not one but two fathers. Dad has had numerous jobs and gotten involved in quick money making schemes. His personal resume with me, my brother, my sister and especially my mother is not picture perfect.

Has he given up and packed it in? No.
Can I learn from this man? Can you learn from this man? Yes.

If nothing else, you can read about a man pouring out himself to help others find the good in themselves. No matter what I think about him and the past, I know that he has always tried to keep the family's best interests at heart. Lastly, Dad has learned about himself. That is why we live. We learn about ourselves so that we can become better people. I hope when you read this book that you can see a man on the up road and on his way to the Promised Land. I hope that you can relate to him somewhere in one of his stories and know that of all the problems he has experienced, something good has come of it. Something good can come for everyone – you just need to know where to look."

" My Father's book is a very simple read for all ages from 11 to 111 years of age. I think everybody can relate to the circumstances in the book. There's everything in the book from debt, alcohol, and drug addiction as well as a few near death experiences that hit us all very close to our hearts. These experiences let you know that in white suburbia yes a family-ours- can make it through just about anything thanks to His powerfulness upstairs! So remember when you think you're down and beat, remember who's got your back, the biggest back up of any born again Christian… The Holy Spirit!!!"

Dustin Brown-
The authors middle child and other son- former cocaine addict.

"This book meant a lot more than I thought it ever could. Within the first couple of chapters I realized how much my family had really been through. We are definitely a lot stronger than I thought we were as a whole. There have been a lot of hard times together. And, though, through most of it I was just a bystander... I am a lot stronger because of it. So thanks guys!"

Cali Brown-
Youngest child and only daughter of the author. Small but mighty.

Contact Information:
C/O The Wealthy Farmer Inc.
Box 22015
RPO Elmwood Sq.
St. Thomas, Ontario Canada
N5R 6A1
thewealthyfarmer@sympatico.ca
In 2008 look for us at
www.thewealthyfarmer.com
We encourage you to contact the mentors and coaches below that we have not only learned from and grown from but also endorse.

Fraser Petley B.A. is an Expert Lecturer in the area of Financial Stress in the workplace and the home
fraser.petley@investorsgroup.com
1-800-541-0977

John Kanary is an experienced positive Christian life coach. www.johnkanary.com 1-905-632-6087

Word Of Faith International Christian Center
www.woficc.com

Westover Treatment Center
www.westover-fdn.org

Catherine Eagan Kingdom Business Inst
www.kingdommillionair.com
www.kingdombusinessassociation.com
www.catherineeagan.com

Kenneth Copeland Ministries
www.kcm.org

Thank you for taking the time to read and be blessed! Upon reading and editing The Wealthy Farmer Diary, I've had the opportunity to release my own cares, by sharing with David some of the most fearsome experiences within my own family with drug addictions. Because of reading his triumphs I was able to share... Your book will open many doors and close many that should be.
God Bless you David, God Bless you!

J. Zuberi
Editor & Chief
Crumbs Publishing